AF248978

Begegnungen
An Architect meets Architects

Alles wirkliche Leben ist Begegnung.
Martin Buber

Werner Blaser

BEGEGNUNGEN

AN ARCHITECT MEETS ARCHITECTS

Birkhäuser – Publishers for Architecture
Basel·Boston·Berlin

Dieses Buch wurde freundlicherweise unterstützt von:
This book was kindly supported by:
MESSE BASEL – SWISSBAU

Translation into English: Mark Walz, Berlin

A CIP catalogue record for this book is available from the Library of Congress, Washington D.C., USA.

Deutsche Bibliothek Cataloging-in-Publication Data

Blaser, Werner:
Begegnungen: an architect meets architects/Werner Blaser. [Transl. into Engl.: Mark Walz].
Basel; Boston; Berlin: Birkhäuser, 2000
ISBN 3-7643-6314-2

Cover: Yumiko & Tadao Ando, Werner Blaser; The Pritzker Architectural Prize 1995 Château de Versailles & Grand Trianon

Alle Fotos von/All illustrations by Werner Blaser

Layout: Werner Blaser, Basel
Litho and typography: Photolitho Sturm AG, Muttenz
Printed on acid-free paper produced of chlorine-free pulp. TCF ∞
Printed in Germany
ISBN 3-7643-6314-2

Inhaltsverzeichnis/Contents

Mein Weg zu den Architekten –
Begegnungen suchen, Beziehungen pflegen
My path to architects – Seeking
encounters, cultivating relationships   8–11
Beziehungen vermitteln – das
Potential der Basler Architektur-Vorträge
Facilitating relationships – the potential
of the Basel Architektur Vorträge   12–13

Paul Artaria	14	Mario Botta	66
Alvar Aalto	16	Tadao Ando	68
Aulis Blomstedt	18	Frei Otto	70
Aldo van Eyck	20	Günter Behnisch	72
Ludwig Mies van der Rohe	22	Santiago Calatrava	74
Jacques Brownson	24	Eduardo Chillida	76
Bertrand Goldberg	26	Jacques Herzog	78
Myron Goldsmith	28	Pierre de Meuron	80
Gene Summers	30	Richard Lohse	82
Frank Lloyd Wright	32	Norman Foster	84
Georg Schmidt	34	Roger Diener	86
Jean Tinguely	36	Nicholas Grimshaw	88
Otto Senn	38	Zaha Hadid	90
Rolf Fehlbaum	40	Livio Vacchini	92
Karl Gerstner	42	Theo Hotz	94
William Graatsma	44	Richard Meier	96
Helmut Jahn	46	Juhani Pallasmaa	98
Phyllis Lambert	48	Renzo Piano	100
Josef Albers	50	Arthur Rüegg	102
Johannes Spalt	52	Stefan Polónyi	104
Alfred Caldwell	54	Richard Horden	106
Max Bill	56	Werner Sobek	108
Ieoh Ming Pei	58	Hans Zaugg	110
Gerrit Rietveld	60	Peter Zumthor	112
Robert Venturi	62		
Charles Eames	64	Nachwort/Afterword	114

Mario Botta, WB,
Maria Botta, Karlsruhe 1995

IIT Studenten in der Wohnung von
Mies Chicago 1952 links WB,
Mies, rechts Waltraut van der Rohe

WB, Norman Foster, Basel 1992

WB, Karlsruhe 1998

Tadao & Yumiko Ando, WB,
Federica Zanco-Fehlbaum,
Rolf Fehlbaum, Basel 1993

Richard Meier, WB, Basel 1996

WB, Eduardo Chillida,
San Sebastian 1989

WB, Philip Johnson, Zaha Hadid,
Weil a.R 1993

Mein Weg zu den Architekten – Begegnungen suchen, Beziehungen pflegen

Auf meiner Reise durch Finnland im Jahre 1949 erlebte ich die horizontale Weite und Unendlichkeit der finnischen Landschaft als Gegensatz zu den vertikalen Felsscheiben und den hohen Bergen unseres heimischen Alpengebietes. Der Himmel spannt sich wie ein riesiger Baldachin über die Flächen der Seen und Wälder. Die Natur lädt zum Meditieren ein, und diese Stille war mir ein Zuhause.
Dann kam der noch größere Kontrast: Amerika, wo der normale Alltag stets im Chaos zu erliegen droht. Dort wurde für mich der ganz eigene «way of life» von Mies van der Rohe zur inspirierenden Insel. Der mächtige Mies mit seinem «väterlichen» Entgegenkommen. Dazu kam seine Ausstrahlung als Erzieher auf die junge Architektengeneration am Illinois Institute of Technology in Chicago. Was er den Studenten mitteilte und vorlebte, war die architektonische Wahrheit. Diese Tendenz und Beispielhaftigkeit war auch für mich bestimmend und wegbereitend. Dieses tiefe Erlebnis blieb bei mir bis heute wirksam.
Ich schätzte die Organik im Schaffen von Alvar Aalto sehr, und besonders nach wie vor seine Möbel. Dennoch kann man nicht auf zwei Pferden reiten. Im Prinzip gibt es nur einen Meister. Die Architektur der geistigen Inhalte, wie ich sie in Chicago kennengelernt hatte, ebnete mir den Weg in meine Selbständigkeit. Im Einfachen und im Wesentlichen fand ich mein Selbstbewußtsein, und ich versicherte mich dieses würdigen Erbes.

8

My path to architects – Seeking encounters, cultivating relationships

As long ago as 1949, when I was travelling through Finland, I experienced a contrast to the vertical rock slabs and towering mountains of our native Alps in the boundless horizontal distances of the Finnish landscape. The sky stretches like a vast canopy over expanses of lake and forest. Nature is an invitation to meditate, and the quietness was a home to me.
Then came the great contrast in America, where normal everyday life constantly threatens to degenerate into chaos. There, Mies van der Rohe's very characteristic way of life became an inspiring island for me. The mighty Mies with his fatherly accommodating manner, his aura of educator for the young generation of architects at the Illinois Institute of Technology in Chicago. What he taught his students and lived for them was architectural truth. This intention and his example played a decisive and guiding role in my life as well, and the profound experience has its effect on me to this day.
I have a great regard for the organic style of Alvar Aalto's work, and particularly his furniture. But you cannot run with the hare and hunt with the hounds. Fundamentally there is only one master. The architecture of intellectual content, as I came to know it in Chicago, smoothed my path to independence. I found my self-awareness in simple and fundamental things, and made this worthy inheritance my own.

Seit Jahrzehnten treffe ich in Chicago mit dem deutsch-amerikanischen Architekten Helmut Jahn zusammen. Immer wieder begann unser Gespräch dort, wo Mies mit seinem letzten Projekt, der Convention Hall – strukturell hochentwickelt, wohl der absolute Höhepunkt seiner Karriere – aufgehört hatte. Helmut Jahn nahm diese Leistung als Ansporn. Struktur und Textur beschäftigten ihn ebenso sehr wie Großbauten, die er als Generalist in eine Gesamtarchitektur einpackte, welche ihn auch für eine gewisse Zeit von Mies wegführte. Mit dem Älterwerden und der zunehmenden Erfahrung kam er kurz vor dem Ende des 20. Jahrhunderts dazu, die Mies-Prinzipien wiederaufzunehmen und in seinen neuesten, noch nicht realisierten Projekten weiter zu entwickeln. Mies hätte bestimmt heute seine wahre Freude daran.

Ein anderer Vertreter einer ausgewogenen Architektur im Sinne von Mies ist der Japaner Tadao Ando. Geist und Materie beleben sein Schaffen. In der Oberfläche, beinahe wie eine «Babyhaut», findet seine Betonphilosopie ihre Ausformung. Seine Leistung ist das Überbringen des Zen-Geistes in seine Raumdurchdringungen. Einfachheit und Stille bestimmen seine Bauten. Was Helmut Jahn in seiner Entfaltung der Struktur erreichte, schuf Tadao Ando mit der ruhigen Klarheit seiner Bauten: das Erbe Mies' auf größtmöglicher Ebene weiterzuführen. In der Stille liegt Schönheit und Verinnerlichung, wonach sich die Menschheit so sehnlichst richten möchte.

For decades now I have been meeting the German-American architect Helmut Jahn in Chicago. Again and again our conversation has taken up where Mies left off with his last project; the Convention Hall, structurally highly developed and without doubt the absolute pinnacle of his career. Helmut Jahn regarded this achievement as a challenge. Structure and texture preoccupied him as much as did large-scale buildings, which as a generalist, he would incorporate into a comprehensive architecture that in fact led him away from Mies for a time. As he grew older and more experienced towards the end of the 20th century, he reached a point where he took up Mies's principles again and developed them further in his newest, as yet unrealised projects. Mies would certainly have been delighted with them today.

Another advocate of balanced architecture as exemplified by Mies is the Japanese architect, Tadao Ando. Spirit and material give life to his work. Surfaces almost like a baby's skin provide the form for his philosophy of concrete. His achievement is infusing the spirit of Zen into spatial penetrations. Simplicity and stillness characterise his buildings. What Helmut Jahn achieved in his development of structure, Tadao Ando created with the quiet clarity of his buildings: the extrapolation of Mies's heritage onto the largest possible plane. In stillness lies the beauty and introspection by which humanity so longingly desires to be guided.

Mies stand meinen beiden jüngeren Kollegen Pate. Sie sind keine Imitatoren. Ihr eigenes schöpferisches Engagement ist maßgebend. Sein Nachlass auf den Ebenen der strukturellen Verpflichtung und der sinnlichen Vertiefung, was gute Architektur sein kann, ist wegbereitend. Es steht jedem ernsthaften Architekten frei, beides, nie das Eine oder das Andere allein, zu seinem Ziel zu erklären. Mies ist tot, es lebe Mies.

An diesen drei Namen: Mies – Jahn – Ando kann man den inneren Gehalt einer Begegnung darstellen, aufzeigen, wie Prinzipien direkt und indirekt aufgenommen und fruchtbar gemacht werden können. Das sollen die hier geschilderten 50 wichtigen «Begegnungen» (tatsächlich waren es in meinem Leben wohl über 100) auf eine hoffentlich anregende Weise dem Leser näherbringen.

Yumiko & Tadao Ando, Werner Blaser; The Pritzker Architectural Prize 1995 Château de Versailles & Grand Trianon

Mies stood as godfather to my two younger colleagues, but they are not his imitators. It is their own creative commitment that distinguishes them. His legacy, on the levels of structural obligation and aesthetic intensification, that can make for good architecture, is ground-breaking. Every serious architect is free to choose both (never the one or the other alone) as his or her goal. Mies is dead; long live Mies.

Through these three names, Mies, Jahn and Ando, the inner content of an encounter can be shown, and we can see how principles can be directly and indirectly assimilated and made to bear fruit. The purpose of the fifty important "encounters" outlined here (in fact there must have been over a hundred in my life) is to make this idea accessible to the reader in what I hope will be a stimulating way.

Beziehungen vermitteln – das Potential der Basler Architektur-Vorträge

Für meine Vaterstadt schuf ich 1980 die Basler Architektur-Vorträge. Damals hatte ich von der Kulturstiftung Pro Helvetia den Auftrag bekommen, eine weltweite Ausstellung «70/80 Architecture in Switzerland» aufzubauen. Es standen anfangs 100 Objekte zur Verfügung; ausgewählt wurden dann 30 Arbeiten, was unweigerlich zu Enttäuschungen führte. Der damalige Obmann des Bundes Schweizer Architekten (BSA), Georges Weber, stellte mir die Aufgabe, ein Forum für Architekturgespräche zu schaffen. Dies gab mir Gelegenheit, nun einige nichtberücksichtigte Schweizer Kollegen zu Worte kommen zu lassen. Darüber hinaus kamen mir die vielen weltweiten Begegnungen zustatten, mit deren Hilfe ich eine internationale Plattform bilden konnte. Die Zuhörer waren neben jungen Architekten und Bürgern der Stadt, die sich über das Architekturgeschehen informieren wollten, auch fremde Besucher. So wurden die Basler Architektur-Vorträge bald weit über die Grenzen zu einem Begriff.
In den verflossenen zwanzig Jahren kam nahezu die gesamte Architektur-Elite aus allen Teilen der Welt in der Kunsthalle, in der Aula der Uni, im Foyer des Stadttheaters und nun seit drei Jahren jeweils zu Anfang des Jahres an der Swissbau in der Messe Basel zu Vorträgen und Gesprächen zusammen. Eine Chance für viele, berühmte und bedeutende Architekten persönlich kennenzulernen.

12

Facilitating relationships – the potential of the Basel Architektur Vorträge

I created the Basel Architektur Vorträge, or architecture lectures, for my native city in 1980. At the time I had been commissioned by Pro Helvetia (the Swiss Arts Council) to put together a worldwide exhibition entitled "70/80 Architecture in Switzerland". There were initially a hundred buildings to choose from, and thirty were finally selected. This inevitably led to disappointments. The then chairman of the Bund Schweizer Architekten (BSA), Georges Weber, set me the task of creating a forum for architectural discussions. This gave me the opportunity to allow some of my Swiss colleagues who had been left out to have their say. In addition I had had many encounters worldwide, which were useful in forming an international platform. The audience was partly young architects, but also residents of the city who wanted to inform themselves about what was happening architecturally, and foreign visitors. Thus the Basel Architektur Vorträge soon became known far beyond our borders.
In the twenty years since then, almost the entire architectural elite from all parts of the world have come together for lectures and discussions in the Kunsthalle, in the university hall, in the foyer of the Stadttheater, and for the last three years at the beginning of each year at the Swissbau at the Basel Messe. A chance for many to meet famous and important architects personally.

Es ist also kein Zufall, daß gerade die gute «auswärtige» Architektur in Basel Halt gemacht hat. Ich denke etwa an Tadao Ando, sein Vitra Trainings-Center in Weil am Rhein, an Richard Meiers Bürogebäude in der Nähe des Bahnhofs SBB und an das Museum Beyeler von Renzo Piano. Bestimmt wird noch mehr Positives der bis heute 175 Redner der Weltelite für Basel beispielhaft werden. Es waren Begegnungen, die nie Selbstzweck waren, sondern den Standard der guten Architektur fördern wollten. Durch die Basler Architektur-Vorträge haben wir mithin erfahren, was Architektur tatsächlich vermag – durch ihre eigene Geistigkeit für eine Stadt die gute Gestalt zu finden.

It is therefore no coincidence that good foreign architecture has come to rest in Basel. I am thinking for instance of Tadao Ando, his Vitra Training Center in Weil am Rhein, of Richard Meier's office building near the SBB station, and of the Beyeler Museum by Renzo Piano. Doubtless there will be further positive contributions from the speakers (175 to date) of the world elite, which will come to be seen as typical of Basel. The encounters were never self-serving, but were intended to foster the standard of good architecture. The Basel Architektur Vorträge have thus shown us what architecture is really capable of – finding the happiest form for a city through its own spirit.

Paul Artaria

1892 Basel – 1959 Heiden (Schweiz)

Nach meiner handwerklichen Grundschulung in Basel studierte ich 1946 bei Paul Artaria: in Abendkursen im perspektivischen Zeichnen und an der Schule für Innenausbau. Erstmals lernte ich so bei einem Meister die Grundlagen des Gestaltens. Mein Training bestand im Erlernen von Maßaufnahmen von klassischen Möbeln und im Verstehen, was die Tradition auch für die Moderne bedeuten kann. Der Basler Pionier-architekt war dann auch zufrieden mit meinen Leistungen, die ich später in den skandinavischen Freilicht-museen auswerten konnte. Er gab mir ein halbes Dutzend seiner Bücher mit auf die Fahrrad-Reise nach Dänemark, um sie dort bei der Architekturelite mit deren Publikationen einzutauschen. Der Kopenhagener Architektur-Professor Steen Eiler Rasmussen sagte mir: «Das Bauwerk soll, wenn es projektiert wird, möglichst seiner Zeit voraus sein, um für die Zeit, in der es dann steht, passend zu sein.» Diese Lehrjahre in Basel eröffneten mir den Zusammenhang für das Gestalten von der Tradition zur Moderne.

14 *Perspektivisches Zeichnen: Aufnahmeskizzen von Werner Blaser unter Paul Artaria, 1948*

Perspective drawing: Layout sketches by Werner Blaser under Paul Artaria, 1948

Paul Artaria

1892 Basel – 1959 Heiden (Switzerland)

In 1946, after my grounding in craftsmanship in Basel, I studied with Paul Artaria, in evening classes in perspective drawing, and at the Schule für Innenausbau. It was the first time I had learned the fundamentals of design under such a master. My training consisted of studying scale drawings of classical furniture and in understanding the significance tradition can have for modernity. The Basel architectural pioneer was satisfied with my efforts, which I was later able to use in the Scandinavian open-air museums. He gave me half a dozen of his books to take with me on my cycling trip to Denmark; I then exchanged them with the architectural elite there for some of their publications. The Copenhagen professor of architecture Steen Eiler Rasmussen said to me: "A building in its project stage should if possible be ahead of its time, so that it can fit in with the time in which it will then stand." These years of apprenticeship in Basel revealed to me the context in which tradition can be adapted to modernity.

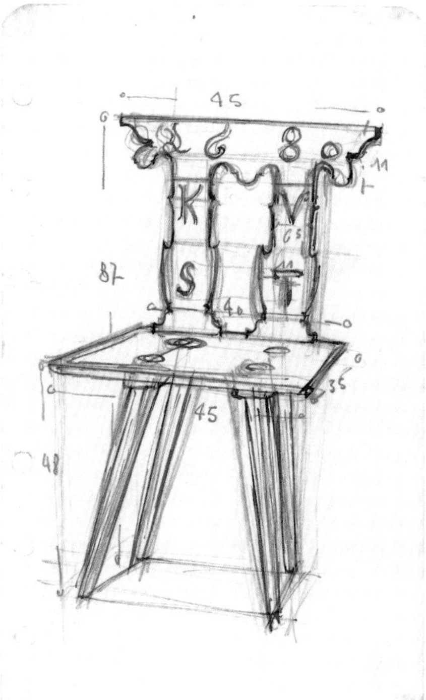

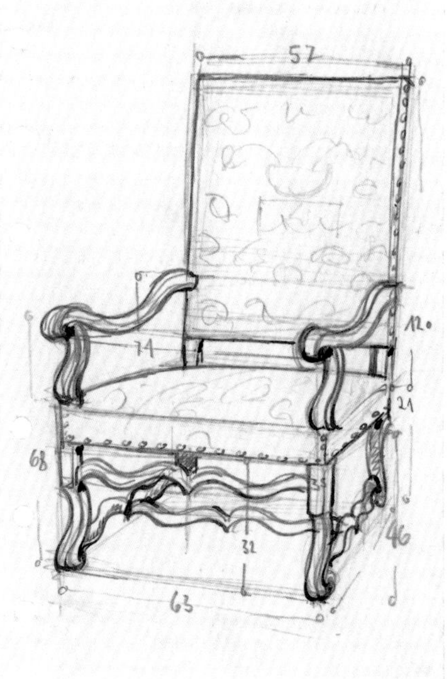

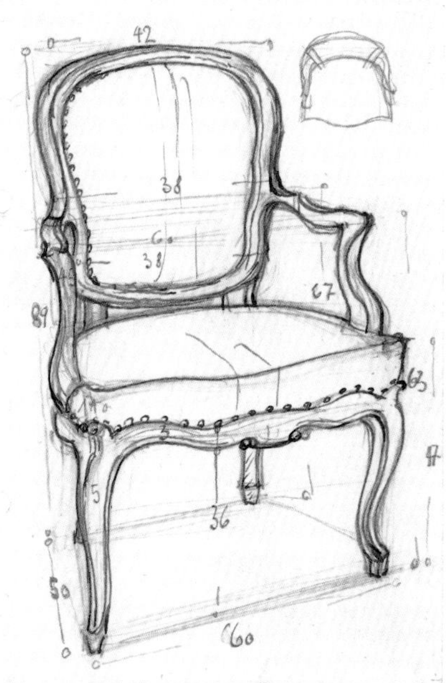

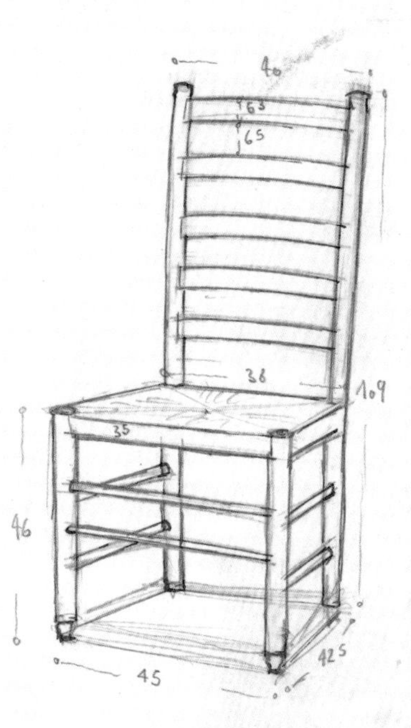

Alvar Aalto
1898 Kuortane – 1976 Helsinki

Es war im Herbst 1949, als ich Alvar Aalto in Stockholm kennenlernen konnte. Natürlich ging meine Frage nach der Möglichkeit eines Praktikums in seinem Büro. Darauf sagte er, daß er jeden Tag einen Bündel Briefe von jungen Architekten bekomme, ich ihm aber trotzdem schreiben solle. Ich schrieb ihm, daß ich auch kommen würde, wenn ich keine Antwort bekäme, denn ich wußte, daß ich wohl keine erwarten durfte. Und so begann mein Praktikum bei seiner Firma Artek in Helsinki. Ich bearbeitete bis 1951 die Einrichtung des Frachtschiffes «Findrader» und die Katalogisierung seiner Standardmöbel. Erstmals war ich in meinem Berufsleben an der Erarbeitung eines Gesamterscheinungsbildes von der Typografie bis hin zu den Einrichtungsgegenständen und zur Architektur beteiligt. Wie unterschieden sich die Persönlichkeiten von Aalto und Mies? Wenn man zum Essen bei Aalto eingeladen war, musste man darben, weil die herumgereichten Gerichte oft bei ihm halt machten. Bei Mies beeindruckte mich sein beinahe väterliches Verlangen nach Wohlbefinden des Gastes.

16
Ausstellung Aalto und Mies: «Möbel in Holz und Stahl» von Werner Blaser, Gewerbe-museum Basel, 1957

Aalto and Mies exhibition: "Möbel in Holz und Stahl" by Werner Blaser, Gewerbe-museum Basel, 1957

Alvar Aalto
1898 Kuortane – 1976 Helsinki

It was in the autumn of 1949 that I first met Alvar Aalto in Stockholm. Naturally I asked about the possibility of a traineeship in his office, to which he replied that he received a bundle of letters from young architects every day, but that I should write to him anyway. I wrote that I would come whether I got an answer or not, for I knew I could not really expect one. And so began my traineeship with his firm Artek in Helsinki. Until 1951 I worked on fitting out the freighter "Findrader" and cataloguing its standard furniture. For the first time in my professional life I was involved in the creation of a complete concept, from the typography through to the fittings and the architecture. What are the differences in personality between Aalto and Mies? If you were invited to dinner by Aalto you went hungry, since the food that got passed around tended to stop in front of him. What impressed me about Mies was his almost fatherly concern for the comfort of his guests.

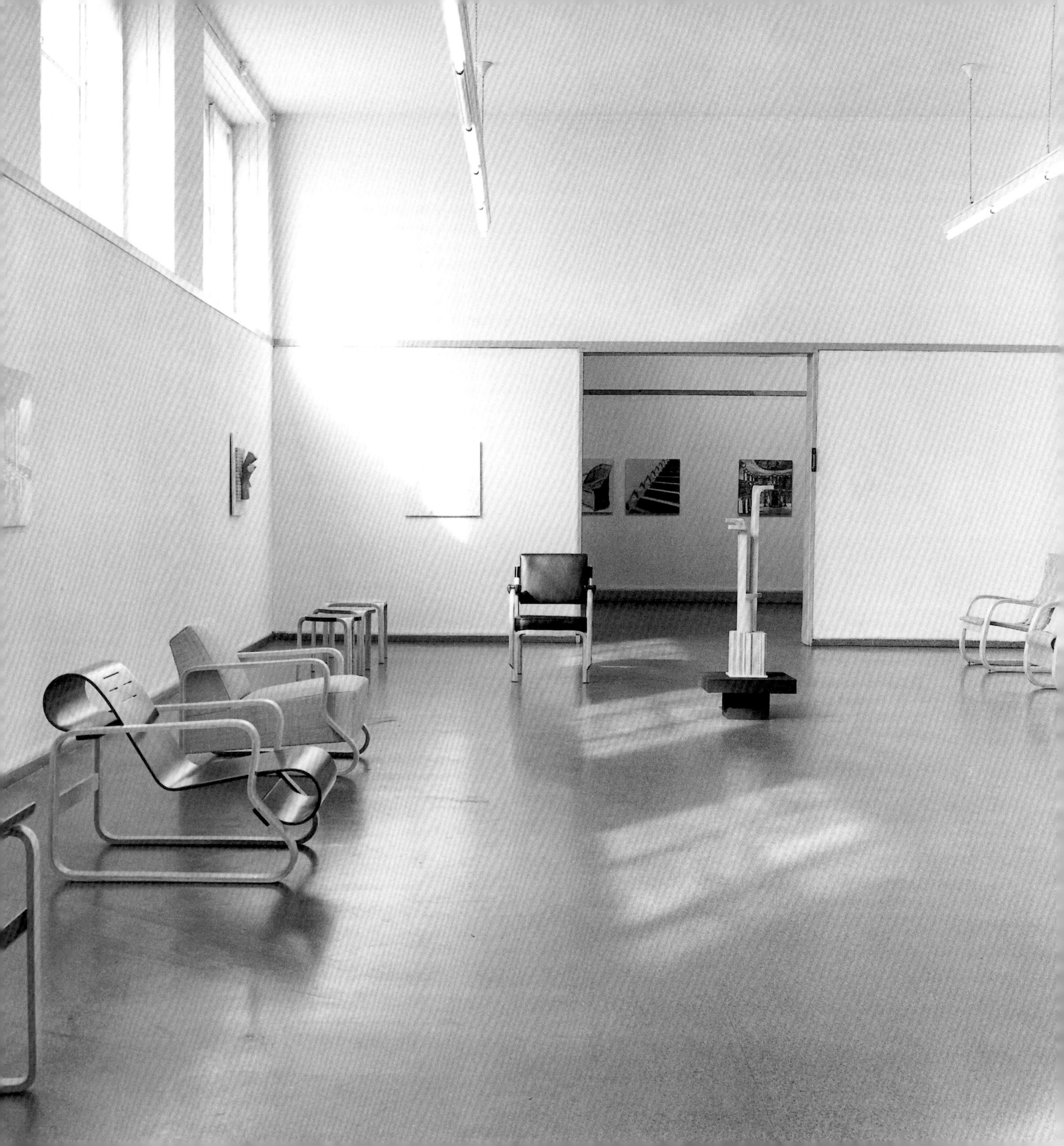

Aulis Blomstedt

1906 Jyväskylä – 1979 Tapiola

Es war bestimmt schwierig, sich in Finnland als architektonische Persönlichkeit neben Alvar Aalto durch-
zusetzen. Die Frau von Aulis Blomstedt war die jüngste Tochter des Komponisten Jean Sibelius; so lag
es auf der Hand, daß Blomstedt die Theorie der Musik in seine Architektur einbezog. Hat nicht Beethoven
einmal gesagt, Architektur sei gefrorene Musik, und dabei denke ich an geordnete Architektur. Bei einer
Begegnung in Munkkiniemi (einem Vorort von Helsinki) hat Blomstedt mir 1950 seine Modul-Forschung
vorgeführt. Schon Leon Battista Alberti hatte versucht, Architektur nach Maß und Zahl zu definieren. Ich
war von Blomstedts grafischer Virtuosität, einem grundlegenden Prinzip der Architektur, fasziniert. Später
hat sein Sohn, Severi Blomstedt, an der Schule für Gestaltung in Basel eine Ausstellung über die geistige
Welt seines Vaters gezeigt.

18 *Canon 60, Maßstudie für standardisiertes Bauen, Modul-Forschung von Aulis Blom-stedt, 1962*   *Canon 60, measurement study for standardised building, studies in harmony by Aulis Blomstedt, 1962*

Aulis Blomstedt

1906 Jyväskylä – 1979 Tapiola

It was doubtless difficult to gain acceptance as an architectural personality in Finland alongside Alvar
Aalto. Aulis Blomstedt's wife was the youngest daughter of the composer Jean Sibelius; so it was an
obvious move to incorporate musical theory into his architecture. Did not Beethoven once say that
architecture was frozen music? Here I am thinking of the language of architecture. At an encounter
in Munkkiniemi (a suburb of Helsinki) in 1950, Blomstedt demonstrated his studies in harmony to me.
Leon Battista Alberti had already attempted to define architecture according to measurements and
figures. I was fascinated by Blomstedt's graphical virtuosity, a fundamental principle of architecture.
Later, his son, Severi Blomstedt, mounted an exhibition of his father's intellectual world at the Schule
für Gestaltung in Basel.

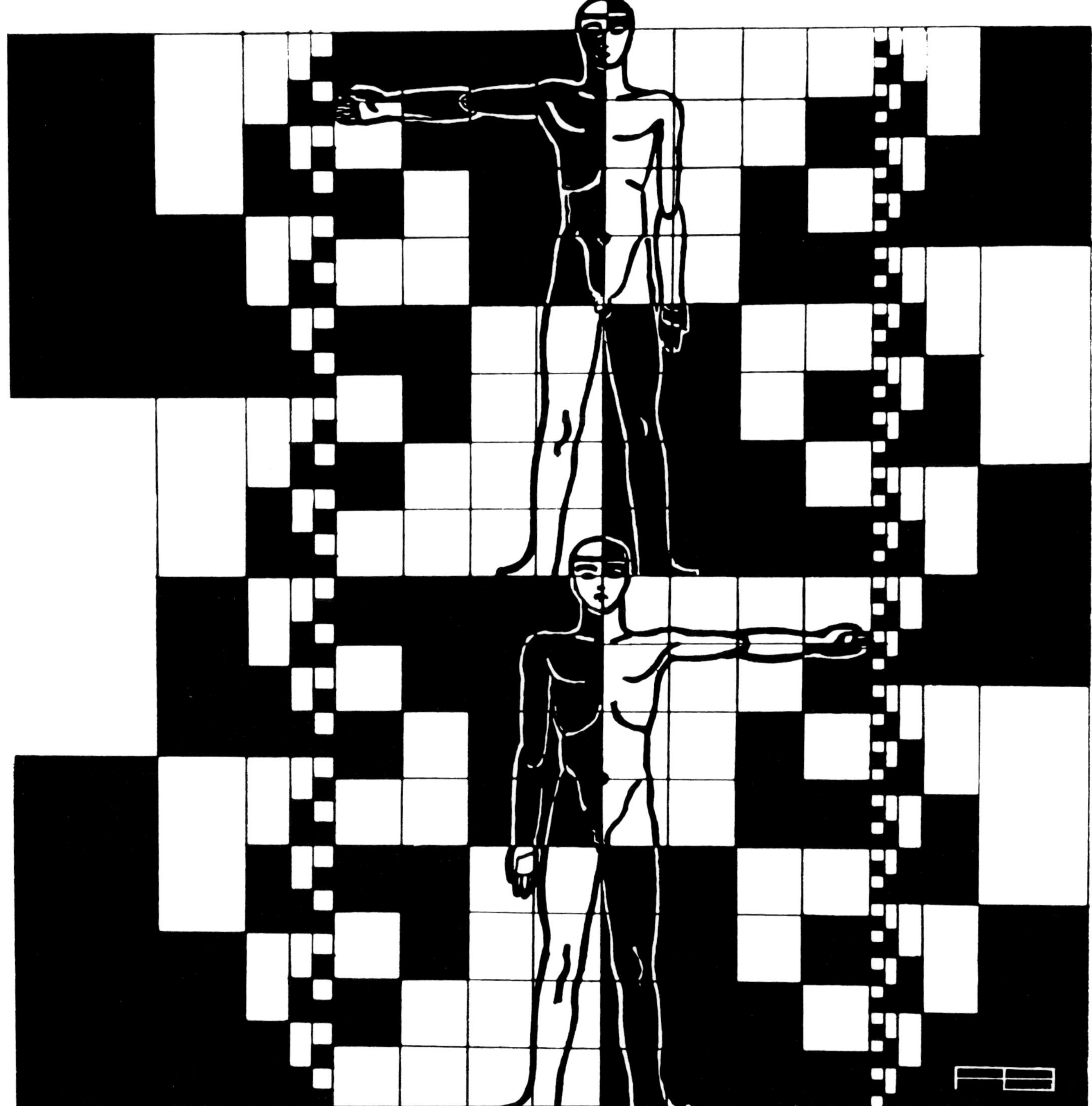

Aldo van Eyck
1918 Driebergen – 1999 Loenen a.d. Vecht

Anfang der fünfziger Jahren, auf meiner Reise von Helsinki nach Chicago, begegnete ich Aldo van Eyck in Amsterdam. Mit Begeisterung erzählte er mir von seinen Reisen und Funden in Afrika. Er fand sich dort bestätigt, auf der Basis der rhythmischen Reihung der Bauglieder in unendlicher Wiederholung gleichgearteter Elemente zu arbeiten. Der erdgebundene elementare Stein als Maß aller Dinge bestimmte später in seinem Schaffen seinen Ausdruck. Eine erstaunliche Spannweite ohne Widersprüche bestimmte im Formalen wie im Stilistischen sein Schaffen. Als Hommage an den Meister werde ich nun mit seiner Frau, Hannie van Eyck, das vor seinem Tode geplante Buch der Ausstellung an der Dokumenta in Kassel 1997«The Enigma of Size», aufarbeiten und veröffentlichen: ein Buch über moderne Malerei, Baukunst und Stadtgestaltung, eine Dokumentation z. B. über heimische Häuser und Siedlungen der Dogon in Westafrika, Pueblos aus New Mexico und Pläne von San Giorgio Maggiore in Venedig.

  Kirche «De Pastoor van Arskerk» in Den Haag, 1964–69

Church "De Pastoor van Arskerk" in the Hague, 1964–69

Aldo van Eyck
1918 Driebergen – 1999 Loenen a.d. Vecht

At the beginning of the 1950s, on my journey from Helsinki to Chicago, I met Aldo van Eyck in Amsterdam. He talked to me with great enthusiasm about his travels and discoveries in Africa. There he had found affirmation for his work in the rhythmical ranking of components in an infinite repetition of identical elements. Earthbound, elemental stone as the measure of all things later determined the expression of his creations. An astonishing breadth devoid of contradictions characterised his work both in form and style. As a tribute to the master, his wife Hannie van Eyck and I will now be revising and publishing the book he was planning, before his death, on the exhibition at the 1997 Dokumenta in Kassel. "The Enigma of Size" is a documentary combining modern painting, architecture and urban design, such as indigenous houses and settlements of the Dogon in West Africa, Pueblos from New Mexico and plans of San Giorgio Maggiore in Venice.

Ludwig Mies van der Rohe
1886 Aachen – 1969 Chicago

Wohl meine bedeutendste Begegnung mit Architekten war diejenige mit Mies, schon im Jahre 1951. Seiner Lehre zufolge können seine grundlegenden Erkenntnisse nicht über das geschriebene oder gesprochene Wort erklärt werden, sondern nur über seine Innerlichkeit; nach Laotse «Wer weiß, spricht nicht, wer spricht, weiß nicht.» Dies war auch konstitutiv für seine Persönlichkeit: Wie er mich etwa in seinem Büro in Chicago 1963 erst nach meiner «Akklimatisation» persönlich empfing und dann 1964 in seiner Wohnung großzügig bewirtete. Die Gespräche über Architektur in deutscher Sprache waren für ihn wie ein Refugium, wie das Zurückfinden zu etwas im inneren Verborgenes. Die Kontemplation als konstitutive Eigenschaft seiner Architektur findet in der fernöstlichen Kultur eine Entsprechung. Darum habe ich das Mies-Fotoarchiv nach Möglichkeit nicht benutzt, um vielmehr durch das eigene Kamera-objektiv seine Wirklichkeit in kompromißloser Konsequenz selbst zu erarbeiten.

22 *Buchumschlag von Werner Blaser «Mies van der Rohe – Die Kunst der Struktur», 1965 und 1993*   *Book jacket by Werner Blaser "Mies van der Rohe – Die Kunst der Struktur", 1965 and 1993*

Ludwig Mies van der Rohe
1886 Aachen – 1969 Chicago

My most significant meeting with an architect was certainly with Mies, as long ago as 1951. According to his teaching, his basic insights cannot be explained through the written or spoken word, but only through its inwardness; Laotse's "Those who know do not talk, those who talk do not know". This was also a constitutive element in his personality: Such as when he received me personally in his Chicago office only after my "acclimatisation" and then generously entertained me at his apartment in 1964. The discussions on architecture in German were like a refuge for him, like finding his way back to something hidden inside himself. Contemplation, as a constitutive characteristic of his architecture, finds a counter-part in Far Eastern culture. I have therefore, wherever possible, not used the Mies photo archive, so as to study his reality myself with uncompromising determination through my own camera lens.

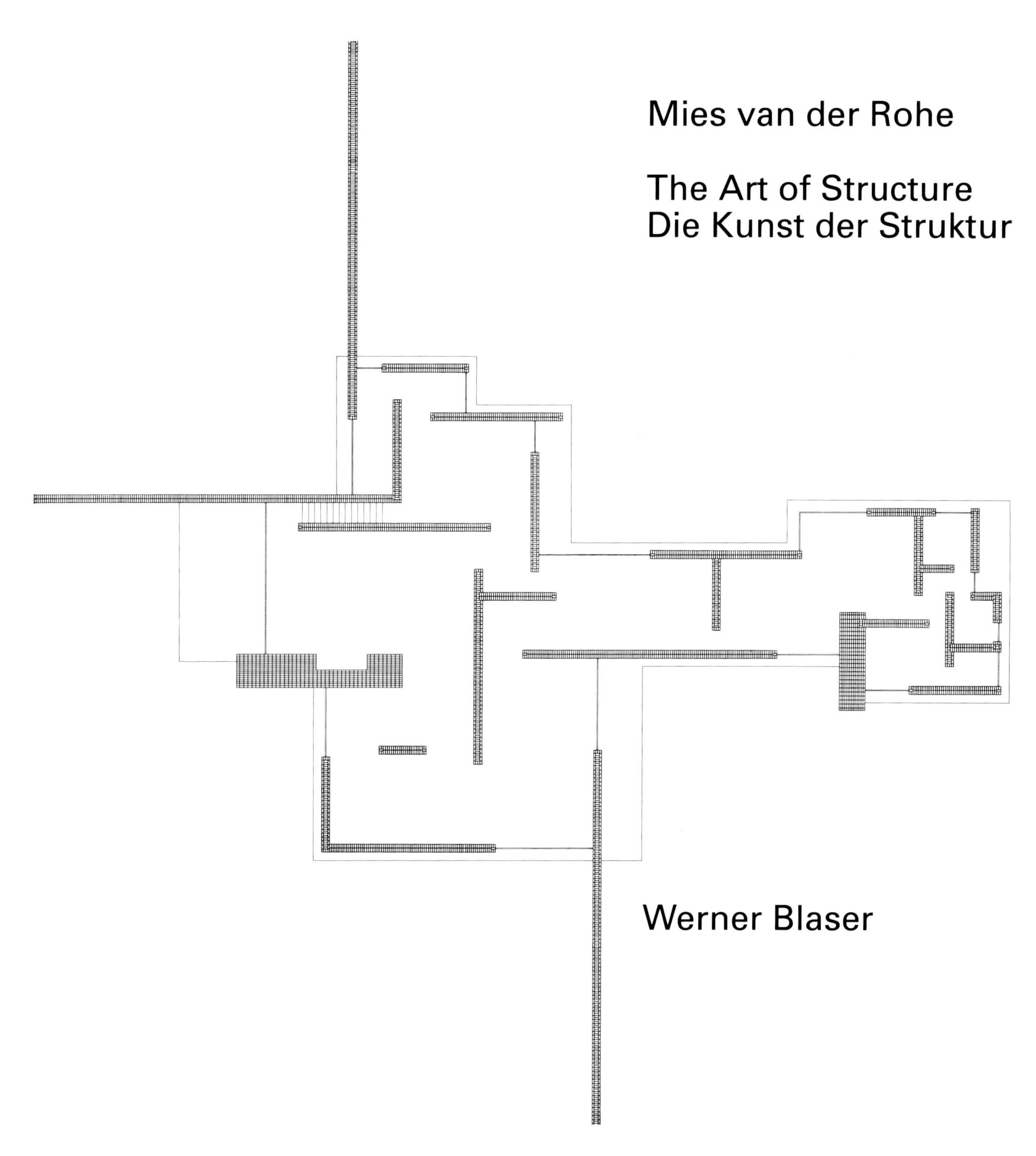

Mies van der Rohe

The Art of Structure
Die Kunst der Struktur

Werner Blaser

Jacques Brownson
1923 Aurora (Illinois)

Eigentlich gibt es nur wenige begabte Mies-Schüler. Jacques Brownson ist einer von ihnen. Sein Haus in der Prairie von Chicago war noch «Mies-like». Schon sein Civic Center in der Loop von Chicago, welches er als «Architect in charge» bei der C.F. Murphy Association ausführte, war im Äußern scheinbar noch Mies verpflichtet, zeugte aber im Innern von einer großen schöpferischen Vielfalt und Unabhängigkeit. Er war sich der Tradition der Chicago-Schule bewußt. Das von Mies angestrebte Werkstattmässige hat er später in Denver im Auseinandernehmen und Zusammenfügen von Porsche-Automobilen praktiziert. Die Hülle wurde sorgfältig vom Motor getrennt – wie in der Architektur ist die Hülle Verkleidung und das Chassis Konstruktion.
Anhand dieser Erfahrung hat Brownson an der Feier zum hundertsten Geburtstag von Mies in Aachen seine eigene Architektur vorgestellt: einer Einfachheit verpflichtet, welche die architektonischen Prinzipien und jene der Natur respektiert.

24 *Chicago Civic Center, 1963–66*   *Chicago Civic Center, 1963–66*

Jacques Brownson
1923 Aurora (Illinois)

There are actually only a few talented pupils of Mies, but Jaques Brownson is one of them, and his house in the Chicago Prairie was still "Mies-like". His Civic Center in the Chicago Loop, which he executed as architect in charge at C.F. Murphy Association, still seemed on the outside to owe a debt to Mies, but on the inside was already showing great creative variety and independence. He was conscious of the tradition of the Chicago school. Later in Denver he practised the workshop style aspired to by Mies, taking apart and reassembling Porsche cars. The shell would be carefully separated from the engine – as in architecture, the shell is façade and the chassis is construction. On the strength of this experience, Brownson presented his own architecture at the celebration for Mies's hundredth birthday in Aachen: committed to a simplicity that respects both architectural principles and those of nature.

Bertrand Goldberg
1913 Chicago – 1998 Chicago

Der Architekt, der am Bauhaus studiert hatte, führte auf dem Bausektor in den Vereinigten Staaten neue Tendenzen ein. Neben meinem Studium am IIT konnte ich in seinem Büro an der Michigan Avenue in Chicago arbeiten: Ich wirkte an der Einrichtung eines vorfabrizierten Hauses, aufbauend auf dem System einer Eisenbahnwagenhülle, für Long Island (New York) mit. Es gehörte zur Persönlichkeit von Bertrand Goldberg, daß ich seiner Sekretärin meine Lohnvorstellung mitteilen konnte. Durch sein großzügiges Entgegenkommen war es mir am Ende meines USA-Aufenthaltes möglich, mein halbjähriges Studium der klassischen japanischen Architektur zu finanzieren. Er hat meine Intentionen als begierig lernender junger Architekt in jeder Hinsicht unterstützt. Später hat er die beiden Wohntürme der Marina City am Chicago River in sichtbarem Eisenbetonskelett gebaut.

Apartment house in Chicago, 1952

Bertrand Goldberg
1913 Chicago – 1998 Chicago

This architect, who had studied at the Bauhaus, introduced new trends into the construction industry in the United States. Alongside my studies at the IIT I also worked in his offices on Michigan Avenue in Chicago: I was involved in furnishing a prefabricated house for Long Island (New York) based on the system used for the shell of a railway wagon. It was typical of Bertrand Goldberg's personality that I was able to tell his secretary my idea of what my salary should be. His generous accommodation enabled me to finance my half-year study of classical Japanese architecture at the end of my stay in the USA. He supported my intentions as an eager young architect in every possible way. He later built the two apartment towers of Marina City on the Chicago River with their exposed concrete structure.

Myron Goldsmith
1918 Chicago – 1996 Chicago

Die Baudisziplin sollte eigentlich mit dem Ingenieurwesen verknüpft sein. Myron Goldsmith war einer der wenigen Architekten, der beide Disziplinen studierte und beherrschte. Er war ganz eng mit Mies verbunden; als «Architect in charge» hat er das Farnsworth House mitgeprägt. Die Freundschaft über Jahrzehnte war für uns beide fördernd in der Auseinandersetzung mit der Moderne. Das überaus facettenreiche Werk dieses von der Ingenieur-Kunst inspirierten Architekten habe ich später in einem Buch, «Bauten und Konzepte», zusammengefaßt. Ingenieur-Architektur ist das Zusammenführen beider Disziplinen zum Gesamtkunstwerk, zur übergeordneten Gestalt im Großen wie im Kleinen. Myron Goldsmith war einer der engagiertesten Architekten; das «Canadian Centre for Architecture» nannte ihn einen «poet of structure». Am Illinois Institute of Technology wirkte er als einer der bedeutendsten Pädagogen nach Mies.

28   *Ruck-A-Chucky Hängebrücke in Colorado, Projekt 1976*   *Ruck-A-Chucky suspension bridge in Colorado, 1976 project*

Myron Goldsmith
1918 Chicago – 1996 Chicago

Architecture should really be linked to engineering. Myron Goldsmith was one of the few architects who had studied and mastered both disciplines. He was very close to Mies, and had a hand in the creation of Farnsworth House as architect in charge. Our decades-long friendship was a support to both of us in coming to grips with modernity. Later on, I collated the very multi-faceted work of this engineering-inspired architect in a book called "Buildings and Concepts". Engineering architecture is the bringing together of both disciplines into a combined work of art, into a higher form that embraces both the general and the particular. Myron Goldsmith was one of the most committed architects; the Canadian Centre for Architecture called him a "poet of structure". At the Illinois Institute of Technology he was valued as one of the most significant teachers after Mies.

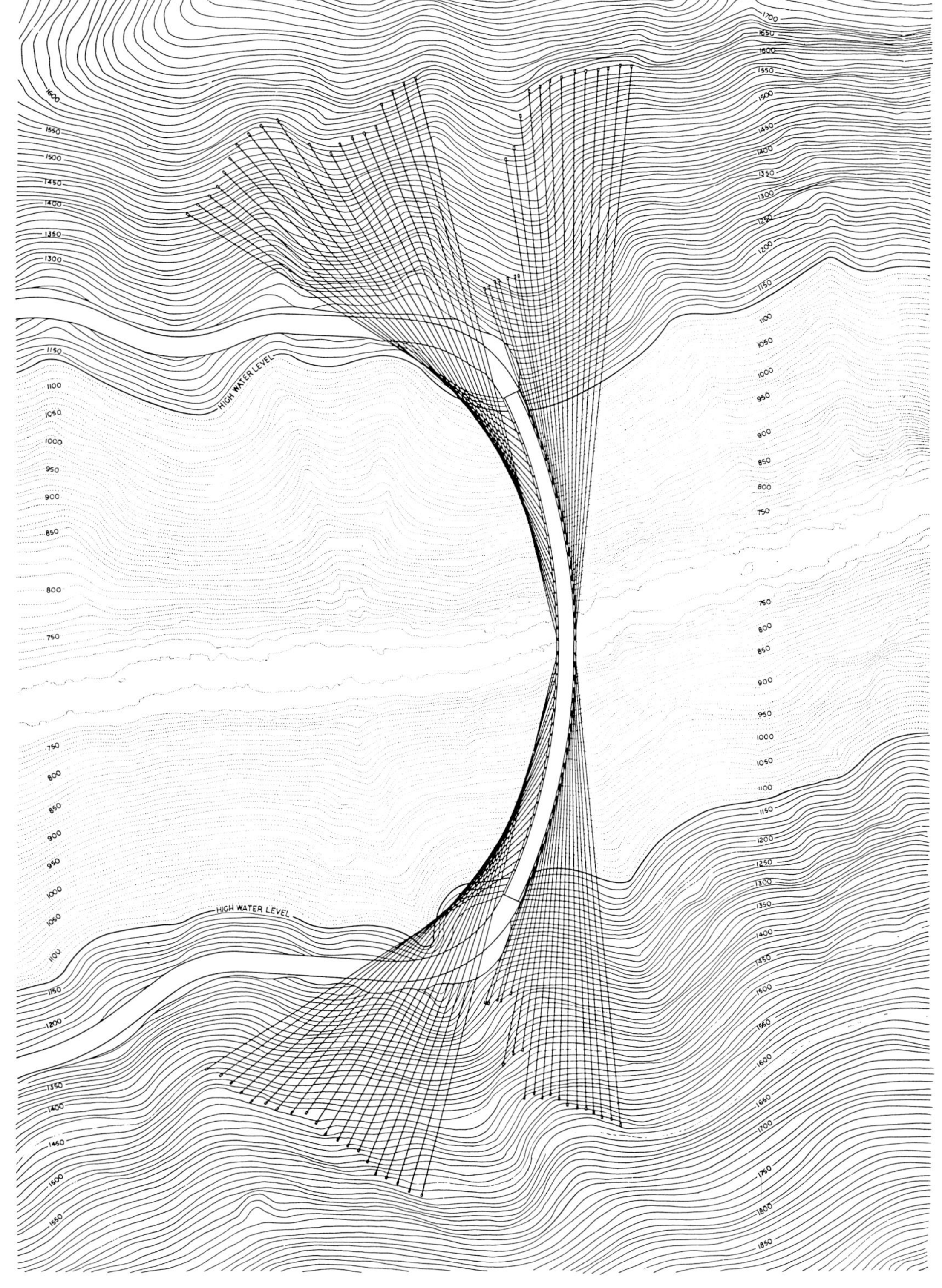

HIGH WATER LEVEL
HIGH WATER LEVEL

Gene Summers
1928 Texas

Einer meiner guten Freunde im Umkreis von Mies van der Rohe war der damalige Bürochef Gene Summers.
Er begleitete mich bei der Erarbeitung des Mies-Buches «Kunst der Struktur». Seine enge Beziehung zum
Meister, seine profunde Kenntnis vor allem der Großprojekte über 16 Jahre, war für mich inspirierend.
Bei seiner ersten selbständigen Arbeit im Büro C.F. Murphy entwickelte er den sogenannten «Universal
Space», eine Mehrzweck- und Ausstellungshalle in Chicago. Später war er in Los Angeles und moder-
nisierte dort unter Phyllis Lambert das vornehme Hotel Biltmore (das spätere Presse-Headquarter der
Olympiade), das er auch als Direktor leitete. Nach Aufenthalten in Südfrankreich kam Summers zurück
nach Chicago als Dekan der Architektur im IIT; dort hat er meinem Sohn Christian den «Master of Architecture» ausgehändigt.

30   *Mehrzweckhalle «McCormick Place-on-the-Lake» in Chicago, 1968–71*   *Multi-purpose hall "McCormick Place-on-the-Lake" in Chicago, 1968–71*

Gene Summers
1928 Texas

One of my good friends in Mies van der Rohe's circle was the then head of the office, Gene Summers. We
worked together on the Mies book "The Art of Structure". His close relationship to the master, his profound
knowledge, above all, of the major projects over sixteen years, was an inspiration to me. In his first
independent work in the C.F. Murphy office he developed what is known as the "Universal Space", a
convention and exhibition hall in Chicago. Later, he was in Los Angeles, and there under Phyllis Lambert
he modernised the exclusive Hotel Biltmore (later the press headquarters for the Olympics), which he
also managed. After stays in southern France, Summers came back to Chicago as Dean of Architecture
at IIT, where he granted my son Christian his Master of Architecture.

Frank Lloyd Wright
1867 Richland Center (Wisconsin) – 1959 Taliesin West (Arizona)

Dem großen Meister der Baukunst begegnete ich erstmals 1951 auf der Straße in Chicago, er trug seinen typischen Hut mit geradem Rand und sein Mantelkleid; ein kurzes Gespräch kam zustande. Ein Jahr danach durfte ich ein Weekend in seiner Sommerschule Taliesien East in Madison (Wisconsin) verbringen, ich nahm Fotos seiner Villen in Oak Park bei Chicago als Gegenleistung mit. Damals hatten die Studenten gerade ein Holzboot für Mr. Wright und seine Gäste fertiggestellt, das für den Fluss, der durch das Gelände zieht, bestimmt war. Wright nannte sich selbst den amerikanischsten aller Amerikaner oder «Usonier», wie er auch seine Wohnhäuser in den dreißiger Jahren als «Usonierhäuser» betitelte. Als Architekt und Pädagoge hat er mit seinen subjektiven Einfällen, einmaligen Experimenten und revolutionären Schöpfungen eine weithin prägende Rolle in der Architektur des 20. Jahrhunderts gespielt.

 Taliesin West, Scottsdale (Arizona), 1938   *Taliesin West, Scottsdale (Arizona), 1938*

Frank Lloyd Wright
1867 Richland Center (Wisconsin) – 1959 Taliesin West (Arizona)

I met the great master of the art of building for the first time on a Chicago street in 1951. He was wearing his characteristic hat with its straight brim and his coat dress, and we had a short conversation. A year later I spent a weekend at his Taliesin East summer school in Madison, Wisconsin, bringing photos of his houses in Oak Park near Chicago as payment. At that time the students had just finished a wooden boat for Mr Wright and his guests to go on the river that runs through the grounds. Wright called himself the most American of all Americans, or "the Usonian", just as he called his houses in the thirties "Usonian Houses". As architect and teacher, he played an extensive part in shaping the architecture of the 20th century with his subjective ideas, unique experiments and revolutionary creations.

Georg Schmidt
1896 Basel – 1965 Binningen

Die Brüder Schmidt, der Architekt Hans Schmidt und der Kunsthistoriker Georg Schmidt, waren in meiner Heimatstadt Basel kulturelle Autoritäten. Sie waren beide in der Lage, den Sinn der Architektur in Worte zu fassen. Ich denke an Georg Schmidt, sein Zuhause in Binningen, an das von seinem Bruder gebaute Einfamilienhaus. Eines Samstagnachmittags, als ich ihn für mein kleines Büchlein «Wohnen und Bauen in Japan» um ein Vorwort bat, sein Arbeitstisch war überfüllt mit Büchern, sagte er mir: «Wie Sie sehen, bin ich überlastet mit Arbeit, und ich kann Ihren Wunsch nicht erfüllen.» Am Montagmorgen bekam ich von ihm einen Telefonanruf, ich könne den Text abholen: «Gern erfülle ich meinem jungen Freunde Werner Blaser die Bitte, diesem von ihm konzipierten Büchlein das Geleit zu geben, denn dieses Büchlein bedeutet für mich die Erfüllung eines drei Jahrzehnte alten Wunsches.» Anläßlich einer Ausstellung meiner neuen Möbel im Wohnbedarf Basel meinte Georg Schmidt 1956, er wisse nicht, ob das Design 50 Jahre zurück oder voraus sei.

34 *Haus Schmidt in Binningen (Basel), 1929 von Hans Schmidt erbaut; Anbau von Georg Schmidt*

The Schmidt house in Binningen (Basel), built 1929 by Hans Schmidt; extension by Georg Schmidt

Georg Schmidt
1896 Basel – 1965 Binningen

The Schmidt brothers, architect Hans Schmidt and art historian Georg Schmidt, were cultural authorities in my home town of Basel. Both of them were capable of expressing in words the meaning of architecture. I recall Georg Schmidt, his home in Binningen, the house built by his brother. One Saturday afternoon I asked him if he would write a foreword for my little book "Classical Dwelling Houses in Japan". With his desk overflowing with books, he said to me: "As you see, I am overloaded with work, and I cannot fulfil your request". The next Monday morning I had a telephone call from him to say I could come and pick up the text: "I am happy to fulfil my young friend Werner Blaser's request to write a preface to the little book he has conceived, for this little book means to me the fulfilment of a wish three decades old". When I had an exhibition of my new furniture in the Wohnbedarf in Basel, Georg Schmidt in 1956 said he did not know whether the design was fifty years behind or fifty years ahead of its time.

Jean Tinguely
1925 Fribourg – 1991 Bern

Es muß um 1950 gewesen sein, als ich Jean Tinguely – den wir Jeannot nannten – im Wiederholungskurs der Mitrailleur-Kompagnie IV/99 zum ersten Mal traf. Wir waren in der gleichen Gruppe eingeteilt und vom Temperament her einsatzfreudige Soldaten. Was aber nicht heißt, daß wir mit dem Zackigen, Militärischen einverstanden waren. Unser Selbstbewußtsein, geprägt von unseren selbständigen Berufen, war im Militär nicht gefragt. Beim Maschinengewehr war er von der Mechanik fasziniert, und mit Begeisterung hat er das Gewehr zerlegt und wieder zusammengesetzt. Bestimmt hat er später daraus Anregungen für seine mobilen Skulpturen geschöpft. Er hatte große Achtung vor den Konstruktionen des Zürchers Max Bill, hauptsächlich aber faszinierten ihn die Drahtbilder des Baslers Walter Bodmer. Tinguelys Meisterschaft bestand darin, ohne Wenn und Aber in einer «abgebrühten» Gesellschaft leben zu können.

Aus dem Katalog der Eröffnungsausstellung Museum Jean Tinguely, Basel 1996

From the catalogue of the inaugural exhibition of the Jean Tinguely Museum, Basel 1996

Jean Tinguely
1925 Fribourg – 1991 Bern

It must have been 1950 when I met Jean Tinguely – or Jeannot, as we called him – for the first time on an army refresher course. We had been assigned to the same group and were enthusiastic soldiers by temperament. This is not to say that we agreed with jingoistic militarism. Our self-assurance, encouraged by our freelance professions, was not in demand in the military. He was fascinated by the mechanics of the machine gun, and enthusiastically took the weapon apart and put it back together again. Doubtless this later gave him inspiration for his mobile sculptures. He had great respect for the constructions of the Zuricher Max Bill, but what mainly fascinated him were the wire pictures of Walter Bodmer, from Basel. Tinguely's mastery lay in being able to live with no ifs or buts in a tough society.

Tin Guely

Otto Senn
1902 Basel – 1993 Basel

Kurz nach meiner Rückkehr von Chicago und Kyoto bat mich Otto Senn, ihm meine persönlichen Erfahrungen mitzuteilen. Auch ihm war durch das eigene Studium die Fundierung der Gegenwart in der Weitsichtigkeit menschenfreundlicher Architektur wichtig. Die Vorliebe für jene klassische Moderne, bei der das bauliche Detail im Zentrum steht, charakterisiert seine künstlerische Persönlichkeit. Der Meisterarchitekt wurde durch seine charismatische Art – in aller Zurückgezogenheit, Einfachheit und Bescheidenheit – gerade für die junge Architektengeneration zur Kultfigur. In späteren Jahren beschäftigte er sich intensiv mit dem Thema des protestantischen Kirchenraums; 1988 verlieh ihm die theologische Fakultät der Universität Basel den Dr. h.c. für diese Forschungen.

Staircase in the residential block Parkhaus Zossen in Basel, 1935–38

Otto Senn
1902 Basel – 1993 Basel

Shortly after my return from Chicago and Kyoto, Otto Senn asked me to tell him about my personal experiences. His own studies had made anchoring the present in the far-sightedness of people-friendly architecture important to him as well. His fondness for the kind of classical modernism in which the constructional detail takes centre stage characterises his artistic personality. The master architect was becoming a cult figure through his charismatic manner – in all reticence, simplicity and modesty – for a younger generation of architects. In later years he concerned himself intensively with the subject of space in Protestant churches. The theological faculty of the University of Basel awarded him an honorary doctorate for this research in 1988.

Rolf Fehlbaum
1941 Basel

Schon früh, im Jahre 1954, wurde ich bekannt mit der Unternehmersfamilie Willi Fehlbaum. In ihrem Reihenhaus an der Benkenstraße in Basel konnte ich das erste moderne Element einer Alu-Lamellenwand einbauen. Damals fuhr ich einen Lancia Appia, welcher die Söhne, im besonderen Rolf, sehr beeindruckte. So vermittelte ich gleichsam Aspekte der Moderne, und es entstand eine Freundschaft. Im Jahre 1988 lud ich Tadao Ando zu den Architektur-Vorträgen nach Basel ein. Rolf Fehlbaum war von den Persönlichkeiten Yumiko und Tadao Ando so begeistert, daß er auf mein Anraten hin, Ando einen Pavillon der Meditation auf dem Vitra Gelände, das spätere Training Center, bauen ließ. Der Schriftsteller Adolf Muschg, den vielfache Beziehungen an Japan knüpfen, hielt dann zur Vernissage im versenkten Innenhof einen Vortrag zu Andos Werk.

Rolf Fehlbaum
1941 Basel

I got to know the entrepreneurial family of Willi Fehlbaum early on, in 1954. I installed the first modern element of an aluminium lamellar wall in their terraced house in the Benkstrasse in Basel. In those days I drove a Lancia Appia, which much impressed the sons, especially Rolf. In this way I provided aspects of modernism, as it were, and a friendship came about. In 1988 I invited Tadao Ando to the Architektur Vorträge in Basel. Rolf Fehlbaum was so impressed by the personalities of Yumiko and Tadao Ando that, on my advice, he had Ando build a Pavilion of Meditation in the Vitra grounds, later the Training Centre. The writer Adolf Muschg, who has links with Japan through a number of relationships, then held a talk on Ando's work at the private view in the sunken courtyard.

Karl Gerstner
1930 Basel

Ein weiterer Kollege auf dem Gebiete von Kunst und Design, Karl Gerstner, lud mich 1955 in sein Grafikatelier an der Malzgasse in Basel ein, um einen Diavortrag über Mies van der Rohe zu halten. Als Bestuhlung holten wir die Klappstühle aus der Pauluskirche. Unter den aufmerksamen Zuhörern war auch der Architekt Hans Schmidt. Bei Karl Gerstner konnte ich meine *mise-en-page*-Kenntnisse wesentlich vertiefen. Zudem war ich an seinem seriellen Kunstschaffen sehr interessiert. Heute finden unsere Gespräche in seinem Farmhouse im Elsaß statt. Dieses sein Zuhause und zugleich auch Atelier, eine alte Mühle am Fluß Ill, ist die Erfüllung eines Kindheitstraumes. Hier ist ein Ort der Besinnung, wo besonders deutlich wird, daß wir Kunst brauchen, um eine lebenswerte Umwelt zu schaffen.

42 *Kontemplationsbilder von 1956–75 im Weishaupt Verwaltungs- und Schulungszentrum in Geroldswil (Zürich), 1998/9*

Contemplative pictures from 1956–75 in the Weishaupt Verwaltungs- und Schulungszentrum in Geroldswil (Zurich), 1998/99

Karl Gerstner
1930 Basel

Another colleague from the field of art and design, Karl Gerstner, invited me to his graphics workshop in the Malzgasse in Basel in 1955 to hold a slide show on Mies van der Rohe. For seating we brought in folding chairs from the Pauluskirche. The attentive audience included the architect Hans Schmidt. Karl Gerstner enabled me considerably to deepen my knowledge of *mise-en-page.* I was also very interested in his serial art. Nowadays our conversations take place in his farmhouse in Alsace. This old mill on the Ill river, both home and workshop to him, is the fulfilment of a childhood dream. Here is a place for reflection where it becomes particularly clear that we need art in order to create an environment worth living in.

Schulungsraum Praxis

William Graatsma
1925 Brucht (Belgien)

Das Universaltalent – Designer, Künstler, Pädagoge, Direktor der Kunstschule in Maastricht – William Graatsma lebt von karger Spiritualität; er findet den inneren Sinn in der Gestalt der Abkehr von vordergründigem Funktionalismus. Seine Arbeiten zeichnet er in Zusammenarbeit mit G.J. Slothouber. Da ihr Land teilweise unter dem Meeresspiegel liegt, haben sich die geistig-schöpferischen Kräfte der Niederländer in großartigen Ingenieurleistungen gegen die Macht des Wassers manifestiert, und daraus ist eine eigenständige Weltanschauung entstanden: Der holländische Beitrag zur modernen Gestaltung kommt von der kubistisch-konstruktivistischen Seite. Meine vertiefenden Gespräche mit Graatsma fanden in seinen Arbeitsorten Eindhoven, Amsterdam, Maastricht sowie anläßlich der Ausstellung «Kubische Konstruktionen» in der Kunsthalle Bern 1972 und in Basel 1983 im Zusammenhang mit einem Architekturvortrag statt.

 Cubic Constructions Compendium, Eindhoven 1970   *Cubic Constructions Compendium, Eindhoven 1970*

William Graatsma
1925 Brucht (Belgium)

The universally talented William Graatsma, designer, artist, teacher, and director of the art school in Maastricht, lives on a frugal spirituality; he finds inner meaning in the form of rejecting foreground functionalism. His work is drawn in collaboration with G.J. Slothouber. As their country lies partly below sea level, the intellectually creative forces of the Netherlands have manifested themselves in tremendous engineering achievements against the power of water, and this has created an independent world view. The Dutch contribution to modern design comes from the cubist/constructivist side. The engrossing conversations I had with Graatsma took place in his work places of Eindhoven, Amsterdam and Maastricht, at the 1972 exhibition "Kubische Konstruktionen" in the Kunsthalle in Bern, and in Basel in 1983 in connection with an architectural lecture.

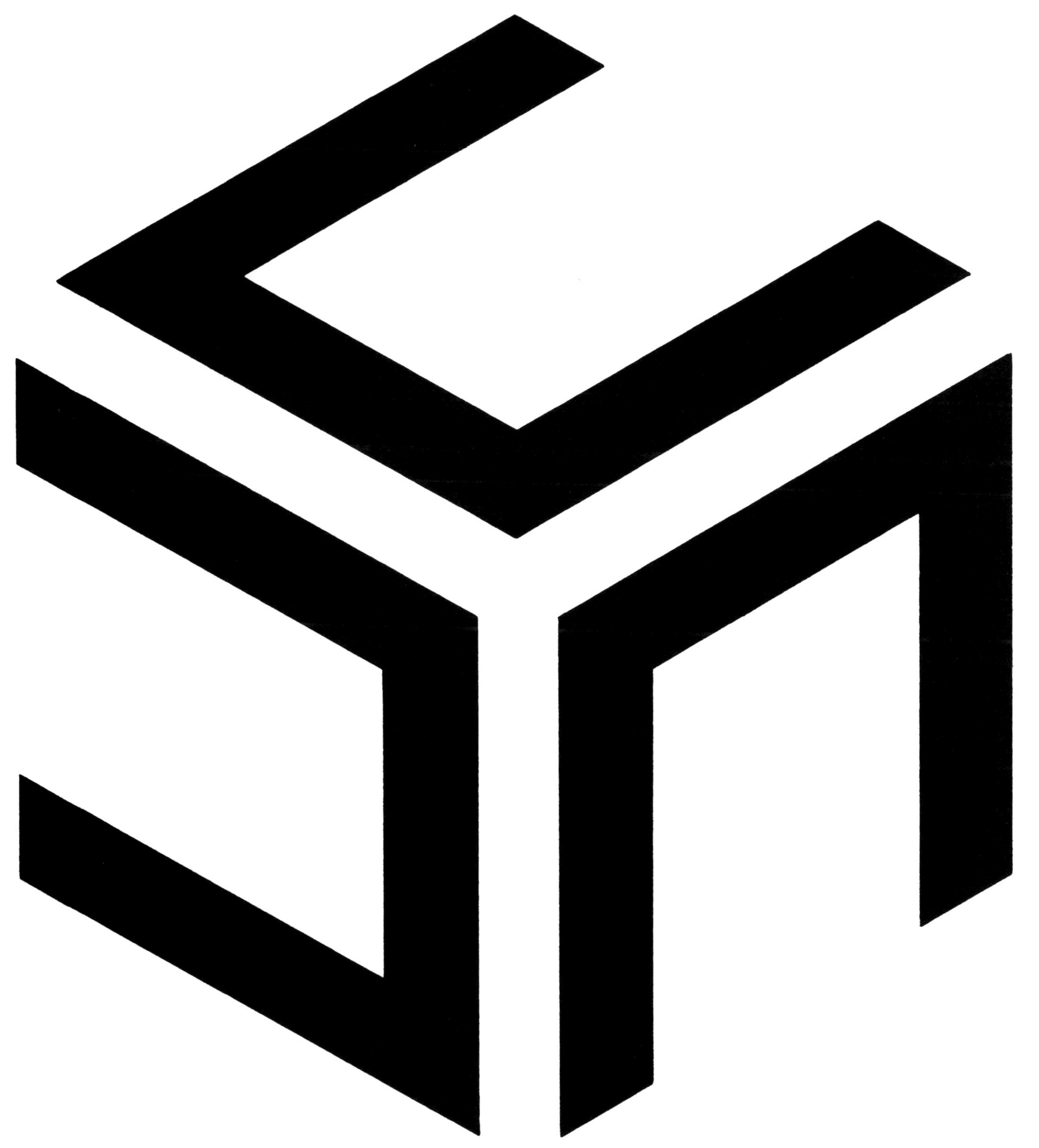

Helmut Jahn
1940 Zirndorf (Nürnberg)

Seit bald 40 Jahren treffe ich Helmut Jahn regelmässig. Die ersten Gespräche fanden im Büro C.F. Murphy in Chicago statt; sie galten den noch nicht erschöpften strukturellen Möglichkeiten von Mies van der Rohe. Von allem Anfang an wollte Jahn aus diesem Erbe seine Gestaltideen aufbauen. Ein erster Versuch war ein Bibliotheksgebäude in Denver. Sein unermüdlicher Mut zum Risiko bewegte ihn zum Kauf der Firma C.F. Murphy Association in Chicago, die er als Präsident heute noch als Murphy/Jahn führt. Kopf und Hand führen seine Skizzen vom Gesamt bis ins Detail. Seit einigen Jahren wird sein konstruktives Talent vom Ingenieur Werner Sobek aus Stuttgart unterstützt. Aus dieser Zusammenarbeit «Archi-neering», wie wir es nannten, erwartet uns eine neue auf das Konstrukt reduzierte klare Architektur, die wohl bald Schule machen wird und zum Besten im Bereich der Ingenieur-Architektur gezählt werden kann.

46   *Airport-Center München, 1989–2000*   *Airport-Center Munich, 1989–2000*

Helmut Jahn
1940 Zirndorf (Nuremberg)

I have been meeting Helmut Jahn regularly for almost 40 years. Our first discussions took place in the C.F. Murphy offices in Chicago; they centred on Mies van der Rohe's not yet exhausted structural possibilities. Right from the outset, Jahn wanted to develop his design ideas from this heritage. One of the first attempts was a library building in Denver. His unflagging willingness to take risks moved him to buy the firm of C.F. Murphy Assoc. in Chicago, which he still heads as president of Murphy/Jahn. His drawings are executed with insight and skill from the general to the smallest detail. For some years now his constructional talent has been supported by the engineer Werner Sobek from Stuttgart. As a result of this cooperation, "Archi-neering" as we called it, we can look forward to a new, clear architecture refined down to a construct, which will soon be the norm and can be counted among the best in the field of engineering and architecture.

Phyllis Lambert
1927 Montreal

Eine der bemerkenswertesten Persönlichkeiten auf dem Gebiete der Architektur und ihrer Vermittlung ist Phyllis Lambert, die ihren Master of Science am IIT 1962 unter Mies abschloß. Ihr war damals ein Zeichentisch im Büro Mies eingeräumt. Als Tochter von Samuel Bronfman, dem Präsidenten der Seagram Corporation, sah sie in Paris in der New York Times das Vorprojekt für einen uninspirierten Gebäudekomplex; sie kehrte sofort zurück nach Manhattan und sagte ihrem Vater, daß er nur etwas machen sollte, was niemand sonst aufzuweisen hätte. Und so wurde Mies van der Rohe mit dem Bauauftrag für das Seagram Building in New York (1954–58) betraut. Ich erinnere mich noch gut, wie sie uns in Chicago im Lake Shore Drive Apartment in ihrer Wohnung im 26. Stockwerk mit Mies zusammen bewirtete und im Gespräch jeweils auch meditative Pausen einfließen ließ. Später gründete sie in Montreal das CCA, Canadian Centre for Architecture, eines der besten Institute dieser Art, dessen Leitung sie bis vor kurzem innehatte.

48   *Apartment-Wohnung von Phyllis Lambert, 860 Lake Shore Drive, Chicago, 1964*   *Phyllis Lambert's apartment, 860 Lake Shore Drive, Chicago, 1964*

Phyllis Lambert
1927 Montreal

One of the most remarkable personalities in the field of architecture and how it is conveyed is Phyllis Lambert, who took her Master of Science at the IIT under Mies in 1962. At that time she was allotted a drawing board in the Mies office. The daughter of Samuel Bronfman, President of the Seagram Corporation, she was in Paris when she saw the preliminary project for an uninspired building complex in the New York Times. She immediately returned to Manhattan and told her father he should do something about it, which nobody else would have been able to do. And so Mies van der Rohe was given the contract to build the Seagram Building in New York (1954–58). I remember well how she entertained us together with Mies in her 26th-storey apartment on Lake Shore Drive in Chicago, allowing meditative pauses to flow into the conversation here and there. Later she founded the CCA, the Canadian Centre for Architecture in Montreal, one of the best institutes of its kind, which she headed until a short time ago.

Josef Albers
1888 Bottrop – 1976 New Haven

Während meiner Tätigkeit als Gastdozent 1956/57 an der Hochschule für Gestaltung in Ulm in Vertretung des Architekten Hans Gugelot, Lehrstuhl für Produktgestaltung, begegnete ich Josef Albers. Er kannte meine Sesselentwicklung in Stahlrohr «All in line» und schlug mir vor, eines seiner Bilder, «Homage to the Square», gegen zwei Sessel zu tauschen. Später dann traf ich Anni und Josef Albers in ihrem Heim am North Forest Circle in New Haven. Sie äußerten die Meinung, meine Fotos von der 860 Lake Shore Drive-Fassade von Mies seien im Flächenraster wie eine Josef Albers-Komposition. Bei ihm geht es um den Versuch, das geometrische Gesamtbild als Ganzheit in Farbe und Gestalt zu erfassen und daraus etwas zu bilden, was Sinn gibt. Besonders beeindruckt hat mich sein Relief mit Ziegelsteinen am Graduate Center in Cambridge (Mass.) von 1962, wo er aus der entfernten Quelle einer altmexikanischen Mauer schöpfend seine Kreativität mit transformierender Kraft entfaltete.

50 *Sitzform aus einem kontinuierlichen Stahlrohr, für Josef Albers. Entwicklung von Werner Blaser, 1960*

Seat in continuous steel tube, for Josef Albers. Developed by Werner Blaser, 1960

Josef Albers
1888 Bottrop – 1976 New Haven

While I was visiting lecturer in 1956/57 at the Hochschule für Gestaltung in Ulm, where I was standing in for the architect Hans Gugelot, who held the chair of Product Design, I met Josef Albers. He was familiar with my "All in line" chair development in steel tubing, and suggested exchanging one of his pictures, "Homage to the Square" for two of the chairs. Then later, I met Josef and Anni Albers at their home on North Forest Circle in New Haven. They gave their opinion that the grid pattern in my photos of the 860 Lake Shore Drive façade by Mies resembled a Josef Albers composition. What he tries to do is capture the overall geometrical picture as a totality in colour and form, and out of this to create something that makes sense. I was particularly impressed by his 1962 relief in brick at the Graduate Center in Cambridge, Mass., where drawing on the distant source of an ancient Mexican wall, his creativity flowers with transforming power.

Johannes Spalt
1920 Gmunden (Österreich)

Für mich bedeutet die Begegnung mit dem Architekten und Pädagogen Johannes Spalt, dessen Ahnen im Nahen Osten zu suchen sind, und die Erfahrung «Wien», ein Brückenschlag zu Osteuropa, wo die Wurzeln in der traditionellen Überlieferung greifbar sind. Beeindruckt haben mich vor allem die klassische Architektur der Stadt Koprivstiza in Bulgarien und das Gebiet Maramures in Rumänien. Auch das naheliegende Burgenland stand ihm beim Bauen Pate. Nicht Kopien des Vorbildes, sondern neu durchdachte Lösungen sollen bei der Begegnung verschiedener Architekturen entstehen. An der Hochschule für Angewandte Kunst in Wien, wo Spalt als Lehrer und Direktor wirkte, konnte ich unter seiner Leitung 1973 eine Ausstellung über meine Arbeiten «Architektur bis ins Möbel» aufbauen und ihn 1983 während zwei Semestern in der Meisterklasse für Innenarchitektur als Gastprofessor vertreten.

52 *Zeichnung aus «Klappstühle» von Werner Blaser, 1982, Sammlung Johannes Spalt* *Drawing from "Klappstühle" by Werner Blaser, 1982, Johannes Spalt collection*

Johannes Spalt
1920 Gmunden (Austria)

The architect and teacher Johannes Spalt, with his Near Eastern ancestry, and the city of Vienna meant for me a bridgehead to Eastern Europe, where the roots in traditional customs are tangible. It was the classical architecture of the town of Koprivstiza in Bulgaria and the Maramures area in Rumania. The Burgenland close by also acted as godfather to his building projects. Not copies of the original, but newly thought through solutions are what should be created when several architects meet each other. At the Hochschule für Angewandte Kunst in Vienna, where Spalt was teacher and director, I put on an exhibition under his leadership on my work "Architektur bis ins Möbel" in 1973; and in 1983 I stood in for him as visiting professor for two semesters in the interior design master class.

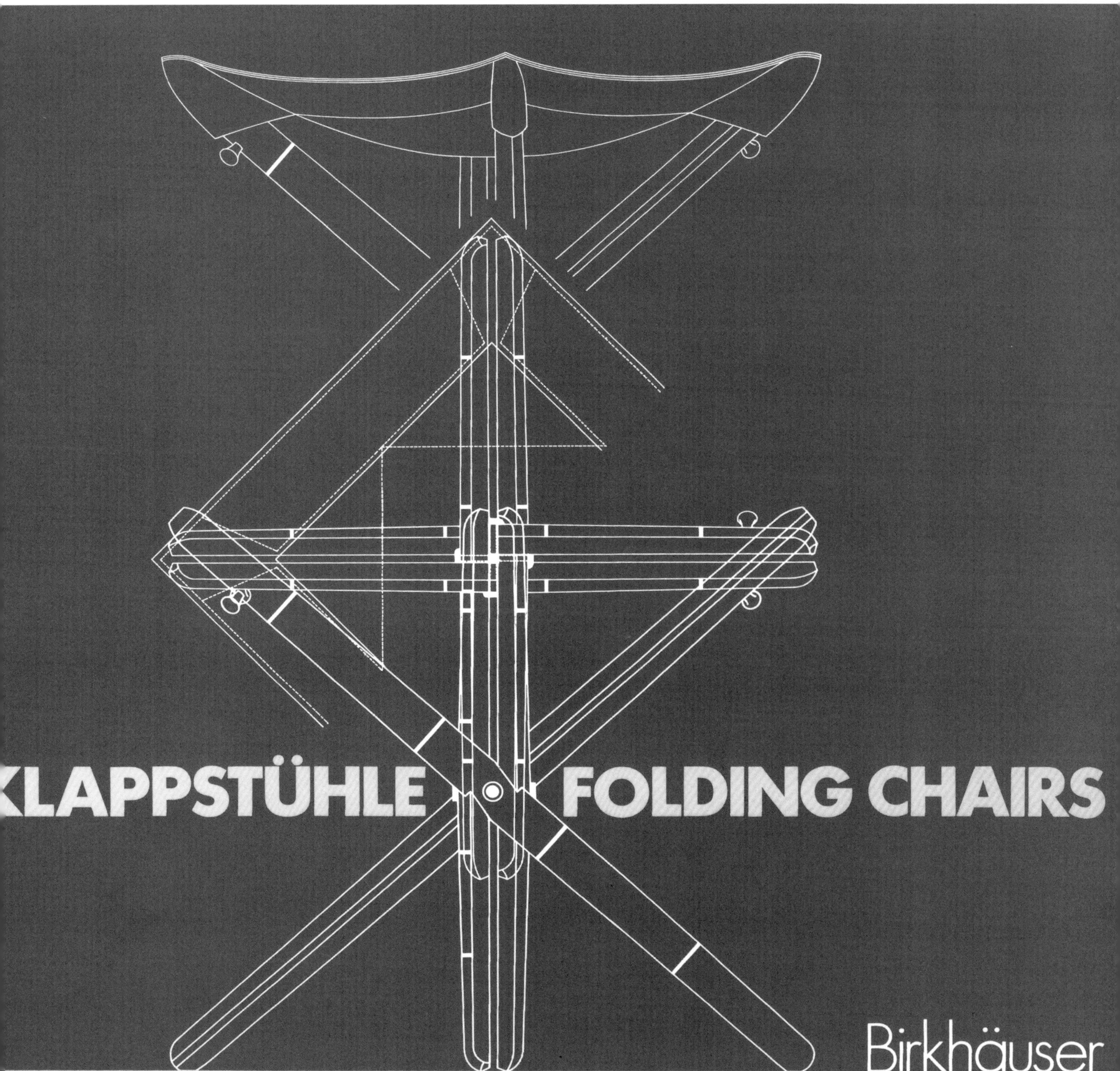

KLAPPSTÜHLE
FOLDING CHAIRS
Birkhäuser

Alfred Caldwell
1903 St Louis (Missouri) – 1998 Chicago

Ich empfinde es als eine Ehre, den heute beinahe unbekannten Alfred Caldwell, vorzustellen. Eigentlich hinderte ihn sein pädagogisches Engagement am Illinois Institute of Technology in Chicago daran, ein größeres architektonisches Werk zu entwickeln, als es sein stilles, aber auratisches Œuvre ist. Von 1947 bis 1997 entwickelte er seine Farmhouse-Anlage in Bristol (Wisconsin) in der Prärie von Chicago, die er selbst als Bauherr, Architekt und mit eigener Hand errichtete. Sein Weg führte über ein Praktikum bei Frank Lloyd Wright in Taliesin East zu Mies van der Rohe am IIT in Chicago. Der Öffentlichkeit mehr bekannt sind seine Landschaftsarbeiten im Lincoln Park «the Lily Pool» in Chicago, 1936, und die Grünanlagen in Zusammenarbeit mit Mies am Lafayette Park Detroit, 1955–63, und Lake Point Tower in Chicago, 1965–68. Die «Zurück zur Natur»-Philosophie, die Innen-Außen-Beziehung als Durchlässigkeit, welche das Bauwerk mit Natur und Umgebung verknüpfte, in Verbindung mit dem Farmhouse-Modell wurde ein geistiger und reeller Ort für Kollegen und Studenten, um über Welt und Architektur zu diskutieren.

54 *Farmhouse in Bristol (Wisconsin) Studio, 1970*　　　　*Farmhouse in Bristol (Wisconsin) Studio, 1970*

Alfred Caldwell
1903 St Louis (Missouri) – 1998 Chicago

I count it an honour to introduce Alfred Caldwell, although today he is almost unknown. Actually it was his commitment to teaching at the Illinois Institute of Technology in Chicago that prevented him from developing a larger body of architectural work than that represented by his quiet but auratic oeuvre. From 1947 to 1997 he developed his Farmhouse complex in Bristol (Wisconsin) in the Chicago prairie, which he constructed himself as owner, architect and with his own hands. His life's journey took him through an apprenticeship with Frank Lloyd Wright in Taliesin East to Mies van der Rohe at the IIT in Chicago. Better known to the public are his landscape work on the Lily Pool in Lincoln Park in Chicago, 1936, a joint project with Mies on the gardens at Lafayette Park in Detroit, 1955–63, and Lake Point Tower in Chicago, 1965–68. His "back to nature" philosophy, the relationship of interior to exterior as a free exchange linking the building to nature and its surroundings, in conjunction with the Farmhouse model, became an intellectual and real place for colleagues and students to discuss architecture and the world in general.

Max Bill
1908 Winterthur – 1994 Zürich

In den Jahren 1955/56 war ich Gastdozent an der Hochschule für Gestaltung in Ulm. Dort lebte ich in einem Atelierhaus auf dem Billschen Campus, einem locker in die Landschaft eingefügten Komplex. Über verlängerte Weekends fuhr ich mit Max Bill in seinem Bentley mehrmals zurück in die Schweiz, erfreut und bereichert durch tiefsinnige philosophische und gestalterische Gespräche. Er war ein Universaltalent auf allen Gebieten der angewandten und freien Kunst. Sein künstlerischer Wahrheitsanspruch, die Konsequenz seiner Ausrichtung wurden zum wesentlichen Parameter inhaltlicher Aussagen, mit denen er selbst die Fachwelt oft zu überraschen wußte.

 Atelierhaus auf dem Areal der Hochschule für Gestaltung in Ulm, 1956
Architektur und zwei Möbel von Max Bill

Studio apartment in the grounds of the Hochschule für Gestaltung in Ulm, 1956,
Architecture and two pieces of furniture by Max Bill

Max Bill
1908 Winterthur – 1994 Zurich

In 1955/56 I was visiting lecturer at the Hochschule für Gestaltung in Ulm. I lived in a studio apartment on Bill's campus, which was comfortably integrated into the landscape. Over many a long weekend I drove back to Switzerland with Max Bill in his Bentley, enjoying and being enriched by profound philosophical and creative conversations. He was a universal talent in all areas of applied and free art. His demands for artistic truth and the consistency of his orientation became the fundamental parameter of weighty pronouncements with which he often surprised even the specialists.

Ieoh Ming Pei
1917 Canton (China)

Chao-Kang Chang (Gropiusschüler) und seine Schwester Pao-Chi Chang (Miesschülerin) weckten mein Interesse für das traditionelle China im Hinblick auf die moderne westliche Architektur. Einer ihrer guten Freunde war I.M.Pei, und so verbrachten wir 1953 das chinesische Neujahr bei einem Dinner alle zusammen in Boston. Das Gespräch bewegte sich im Spannungsfeld Ferner Osten und Moderne. 1998, beim Empfang im Weißen Haus für Pritzker-Preisträger Renzo Piano, begegneten wir uns erneut. Selten hat ein Meisterarchitekt sein berufliches Selbstverständnis zwischen den beiden Kulturen Orient und Okzident so realitätsnah zu überliefern verstanden wie Pei. In meiner Ausstellung «West meets East» 1999 habe ich diese Problematik wie folgt umschrieben: «Die Architektur der westlichen und östlichen Welt ist so verschieden, daß ihr Verhältnis zueinander nur als wechselseitiges Geben und Nehmen verstanden werden kann, ohne daß Eigenheiten aufgegeben werden.» Eine wichtige Partner-Persönlichkeit von Pei war James Freed, der frühere Dekan vom IIT in Chicago, mit dem ich mich immer wieder zu Architektur-Gesprächen zusammenfand.

Ieoh Ming Pei
1917 Canton (China)

Chao-Kang Chang (a pupil of Gropius) and his sister Pao-Chi Chang (a pupil of Mies) awoke my interest in the traditional China in relation to modern Western architecture. One of their good friends was I.M. Pei, which was how in 1953 we all spent the Chinese New Year together at a dinner in Boston. The conversation was about the relationship between the Far East and modernity. In 1998 we met again at the White House reception for the Pritzker prizewinner Renzo Piano. Seldom has a master architect had the facility of conveying his professional self-conception between the two cultures of East and West as closely to reality as Pei. In my exhibition "West Meets East" in 1999 I outlined the problem in this way: "The architecture of the Western and Eastern Worlds is so different that their relationship to one another can only be understood as a reciprocal giving and taking without either giving up any idiosyncrasies". An important partner of Pei's was James Freed, the former Dean of IIT in Chicago, whom I often met for architectural discussions.

Gerrit Rietveld
1888 Utrecht – 1964 Utrecht

Zwei Pionierarchitekten, die ich sehr verehre, bin ich persönlich nie begegnet: Le Corbusier und Gerrit Rietveld. Und doch stehe ich dem letztgenannten auf eine ganz eigene Weise sehr nah. Durch seinen Schreiner, G.A. van de Groenekan in Utrecht, der Möbel nur über den Meister ausführen durfte, konnte ich 8 Original-Rietveld-Modelle erwerben; das Buffet mit 185 Einzelteilen in meiner Sammlung wurde vom früheren Lehrling hergestellt. Ein Zig-Zag-Stuhl ist von Gerrit Rietveld signiert. Das Brett- und Stab-Prinzip bildet den Grund meiner großen Passion zu diesem Möbel-Pionier. Seine Nähe zum Detail im zerlegbaren japanischen Teezeremonie-Möbel des 18. Jh. ist offensichtlich. Die einfache Wahrhaftigkeit dieses objektiven Mobiliars wirkt erzieherisch. Sie sind Raum-greifend und Raum-bestimmend – gleichsam besitzbare Architektur – und eigentliche Kunstwerke.

60 *Zig-Zag-Stuhl, 1934 (signiert; Sammlung Werner Blaser)*   *Zig-Zag Stoel, 1934 (signed; Werner Blaser collection)*

Gerrit Rietveld
1888 Utrecht – 1964 Utrecht

Two pioneering architects I greatly admire but have never met personally: Le Corbusier and Gerrit Rietveld. And yet in a strange way I am very close to the latter. Through his carpenter, G.A. van de Groenekan in Utrecht, who was only allowed to make furniture for the master, I managed to acquire eight original Rietveld models; the sideboard with 185 component parts in my collection was made by the former apprentice. One zigzag chair is signed by Gerrit Rietveld. The reason for my great passion for this pioneering furniture designer is the board and bar principle. Its closeness to the detail in the dismountable Japanese tea ceremony furniture of the 18th century is obvious. The simple truthfulness of this objective furniture has an educational effect. The pieces appropriate and determine the space around them – architecture for sitting on, as it were – and are, in fact, works of art.

ZIGZAG STOEL
ONTWORPEN
1934
Rietveld

Robert Venturi
1925 Philadelphia

Nach meiner Auffassung gibt es, generell gesprochen, gleichsam zwei Architekturrichtungen, die Krummen und die Geraden, man könnte ihnen Höhle und Zelt zuordnen. Obwohl ich bei den Geraden beheimatet bin, kann ich die Krummen nicht ignorieren. Nicht zuletzt durch sein Buch «Complexity and Contradiction in Architecture» wurde Venturi 1966 einer der führenden postmodernen Architekten. In Philadelphia, wo er zusammen mit seiner Frau, der Architektin Denise Scott Brown, lebt und arbeitet und ich 1978 ein Studio an der Architekturabteilung der Universität leitete, fand eine Begegnung in seinem Hause statt. Seine Thesen «Architecture in Transition» fanden bei mir geneigtes Gehör, eine Architektur, die sich über die Norm erhaben hat und versucht, eigene Wege zu gehen, ohne mit der Tradition zu brechen. Mir scheint, daß Venturi frei von Sachzwängen ist und darum die Probleme der Gestaltung individuell aufgreift.

«Benjamin Franklin Court» an der Market Street in Philadelphia 1972–76: Nachbildung Baugerüst seines Hauses aus dem 18. Jh.

"Benjamin Franklin Court" on Market Street in Philadelphia 1972–76: copy of the scaffolding for his 18th-century house

Robert Venturi
1925 Philadelphia

Generally speaking, there are in my opinion two architectural directions, as it were, the crooked and the straight; the one could be associated with caves, the other with tents. Although my metier is the straight, I cannot ignore the crooked. Not least through his book "Complexity and Contradiction in Architecture", in 1966 Venturi became one of the leading postmodern architects. We met at his house in Philadelphia, where he lives and works together with his wife, the architect Denise Scott Brown, and where in 1978 I led a studio in the university's architecture department. His "Architecture in Transition" theses found a ready response in me to an architecture which is beyond the norm and attempts to go its own way without breaking with tradition. Venturi seems to me to be free of material constraints and therefore able to take up the problems of design in an individual way.

Charles Eames
1907 St Louis (Missouri) – 1978 St Louis (Missouri)

Während meines Studiums am Institute of Design (New Bauhaus, Illinois Institute of Technology) in Chicago, beeindruckte mich Charles Eames 1952 mit einem Vortrag zum Thema vom Spielzeug zum Hausbau. Im Jahre 1982 traf ich im Museum of Modern Art in New York seine Frau und künstlerische Mitarbeiterin Ray Eames. Einige Tage später wurde ich zum Frühstück in ihr Haus, das von ihnen entwickelte Case Study House, in Venice bei Santa Monica eingeladen. Dort durfte ich ganz alleine während eines vollen Tages das Haus innen und außen fotografieren. Das hoch über dem Ozean gelegene Wohn- und Studiohaus ist eines der schönsten Wohnhäuser des 20. Jahrhunderts. Es ist aus einem dünnen Stahlskelett konstruiert, mit Standard-Stahlfenstern; die einzelnen Felder sind mit dünnen buntfarbigen Elementen ausgefüllt. Es erinnert in der optischen Leichtigkeit und in der proportionalen Gliederung an das japanische Wohnhaus: es kann beliebig geöffnet, geschlossen, erweitert und verkleinert werden.

<table>
<tr><td>64</td><td>Eames House, Pacific Palisades (California), 1945–49</td><td>Eames House, Pacific Palisades (California), 1945–49</td></tr>
</table>

Charles Eames
1907 St Louis (Missouri) – 1978 St Louis (Missouri)

During my studies at the Institute of Design (New Bauhaus, Illinois Institute of Technology) in Chicago, Charles Eames impressed me with a lecture in 1952 on the subject "From Plaything to House-Building". In 1982 I met his wife and artistic collaborator Ray Eames in the Museum of Modern Art in New York. Some days later I was invited to breakfast at her house, the Case Study House, which they developed together, in Venice near Santa Monica. There I was allowed to spend the entire day completely alone, photographing the house inside and out. The combined house and studio high over the ocean is one of the most beautiful houses of the twentieth century. It is constructed of a thin steel skeleton with standard steel windows. The individual sections are filled in with thin multicoloured elements. Its visual lightness and proportional arrangement are reminiscent of a Japanese house; it can be opened, closed, extended or reduced at will.

Mario Botta
1943 Mendrisio

Meine erste Begegnung mit dem Tessiner Architekten fand im Flugzeug von Zürich nach Wien statt; von der Kulturstiftung Pro Helvetia hatte ich den Auftrag, weltweit eine Wanderausstellung samt Vorträgen zu organisieren: «70/80 Architecture in Switzerland». Später traf ich ihn bei den Basler Architektur Vorträgen in der Kunsthalle, wo so viele Zuhörer erschienen, daß sein Vortrag am gleichen Abend bei vollem Haus wiederholt werden mußte. Harmonie und Schönheit haben für das menschliche Leben ebensoviel Gewicht wie Funktionalität und Nützlichkeit. Mario Botta hat mit der Gründung der neuen Architekturschule in Mendrisio seinen kulturell-politischen Einfluß zum Wohl seiner Tessiner Mitbürger sinnvoll eingesetzt.

66 *Museum Jean Tinguely in Basel, 1991–96*   *The Jean Tinguely Museum in Basel, 1991–96*

Mario Botta
1943 Mendrisio

My first encounter with this Ticino architect took place on a flight from Zurich to Vienna; I had been commissioned by Pro Helvetia to organise a travelling exhibition with lectures, entitled "70/80 Architecture in Switzerland". Later I met him at the Basel Architektur Vorträge in the Kunsthalle, where so many people turned up to hear him that his lecture had to be repeated the same evening with a full house. Harmony and beauty carry as much weight in our lives as functionality and usefulness. With the founding of the new architectural school in Mendrisio, Mario Botta has applied his cultural and political influence for the benefit of his Ticino compatriots.

Tadao Ando
1941 Osaka

Die Begegnung mit Tadao Ando war immer auch eine Begegnung mit seiner Frau Yumiko. Dadurch wurde eine Konversation auf Englisch gewährleistet. Interessant ist, wie er seine Gäste in einem Geschoß eines Apartmenthauses in Osaka unterbringt, wie er mit wenigen architektonischen Eingriffen viel erreicht. Ando kennt keine Wichtigtuerei oder spricht auch nicht über Rampenlichtgrößen. Man kann sagen, daß er über jenes Maß an Zurückhaltung verfügt, die den wahren Architekten mit Innerlichkeit auszeichnet. Im Fernen Osten hat Meditation noch eine lebensformende Kraft, sie weist dem Menschen seine Möglichkeiten und Grenzen zu, das Wesen seiner Aufgabe. Eines seiner letzten Projekte (es wurde von mir in einer Publikation dokumentiert) ist das Museum für Weltkulturen im Rhein: durch eine Brücke der Kunst wird Harmonie und Versöhnung geschaffen. Derzeit beschäftigt mich besonders der Aspekt «der Stille» in Tadao Andos Architektur.

Tadao Ando
1941 Osaka

An encounter with Tadao Ando was always also an encounter with his wife Yumiko, who enabled us to converse in English. What is interesting is how he houses his guests in one storey of an apartment house in Osaka, how he achieves much with a minimum of architectonic intervention. Ando is devoid of pomposity, and does not talk of spectacular dimensions. One could say he possesses that degree of modesty which distinguishes the true architect with inner depth. In the Far East, meditation still has a life-forming power, it shows a person his or her possibilities and limits, the essence of their task. One of his last projects (documented by me in a publication) is the Museum für Weltkulturen im Rhein: a bridge of art creates harmony and reconciliation. Currently, I am particularly interested in the aspect of "stillness" in Tadao Ando's architecture.

Frei Otto

1925 Siegmar (Sachsen)

Die Bemühungen von Frei Otto gelten der Rettung dessen, was einst ein faßbares, klar verständliches ästhetisches Universum ausdrückte. So hat er seine Fähigkeit, Eigenes, Ästhetisches aus der Natur zu kreieren, als Wegweiser für zukünftige Generationen aufgestellt. Seine umfassenden Arbeiten mit «Natürlichen Bauformen», die Experimente aus seinem Institut für leichte Flächentragwerke an der Universität Stuttgart erhielten weltweite Anerkennung. Begegnungen in seinem Wohnatelier in Leonsberg bei Stuttgart und anläßlich der Basler Architektur Vorträge bestärkten mich in der Einsicht, daß kontemplative Erfahrung auf der Wechselwirkung von sinnlicher Wahrnehmung und dem Bewußtsein von äußerer und innerer Gestalt vollzogen wird.

70

Dach für das Olympische Stadion in München 1972, eine Zusammenarbeit mit Günter Behnisch

Roof for the Olympic Stadium in Munich 1972, a joint project with Günter Behnisch

Frei Otto

1925 Siegmar (Saxony)

The efforts of Frei Otto are directed towards saving something that once expressed a tangible, clearly comprehensible aesthetic universe. He has set up his ability to create something personal and aesthetic out of nature as a signpost for future generations. His comprehensive work with "Modulated Coordination", the experiments from his Institut für leichte Flächentragwerke at the University of Stuttgart, received worldwide recognition. Meetings in his workshop in Leonsberg near Stuttgart, and during the Basel Architektur Vorträge, strengthened me in the view that contemplative experience is consummated in the interaction between sensual perception and the consciousness of outer and inner form.

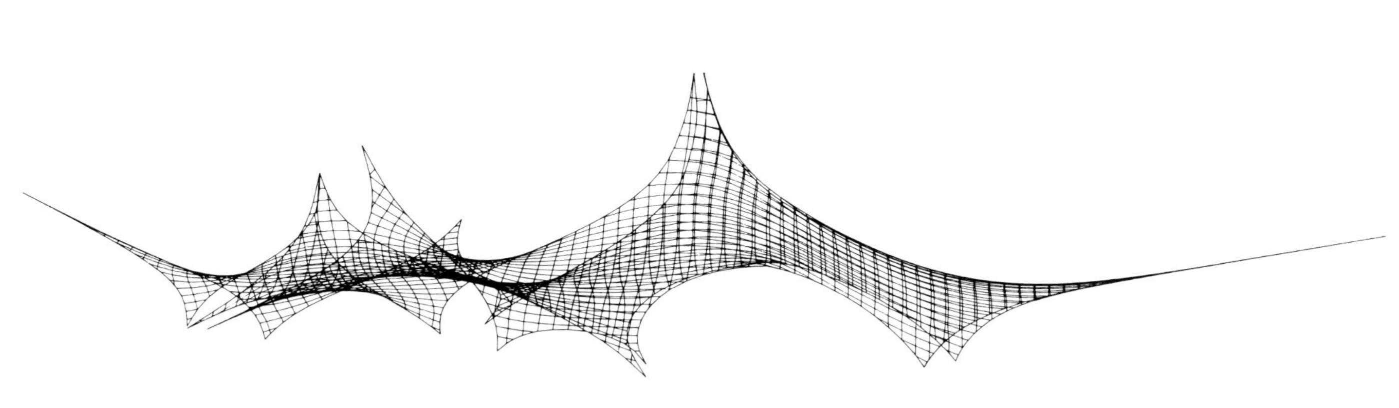

Günter Behnisch
1922 Lockwitz (Dresden)

Die große Leistung von Günter Behnisch liegt im Streben nach autonomer Architektur, indem er auch den Blick für das Optische im Alltäglichen öffnete. So etwa in seiner schwebenden Zeltarchitektur für die Bauten der Olympischen Spiele in München 1972, die mit Frei Otto entwickelt wurden. Behnisch bediente sich der Natur als Maßstab für die Wahrhaftigkeit eines Bauwerk-Ensembles. Ich begegnete ihm bei den Basler Architektur Vorträgen und an der Tagung zum hundertsten Geburtstag von Mies in dessen Geburts- ort Aachen. Behnischs Vorträge sind dem Zeitgeist verpflichtet, der in seinem Schaffen jenes hohe Niveau erreicht hat, das durch den Zauber des Ideenreichtums und die Nuancen der dynamischen Gestalt über- zeugt. Behnisch hat eigentlich alle Stufen, von der naturnahen bis zur dekonstruktiven Architektur, durch- laufen und ähnlich Pablo Picasso jeweils darin schöpferische Höhepunkte erreicht.

72 *Bauten für die Olympischen Spiele in München, 1972*   *Buildings for the Olympic Games in Munich, 1972*

Günter Behnisch
1922 Lockwitz (Dresden)

Günther Behnisch's great achievement lies in his striving for autonomous architecture, whereby he has also opened people's eyes to the visual qualities of everyday things. This is the case, for instance, with his floating tent architecture in the buildings for the 1972 Olympic Games in Munich, which were developed with Frei Otto. Behnisch used nature as a measure of truthfulness in a building ensemble. I met him at the Basel Architektur Vorträge and the conference on Mies's hundredth birthday in his native city of Aachen. Behnisch's lectures are committed to the zeitgeist, which in his work has reached the kind of high level that convinces by the richness of its ideas and its nuances of dynamic form. Behnisch has in fact pro- gressed through all the stages from naturalistic to deconstructive architecture, and like Pablo Picasso, has reached creative peaks in each of them.

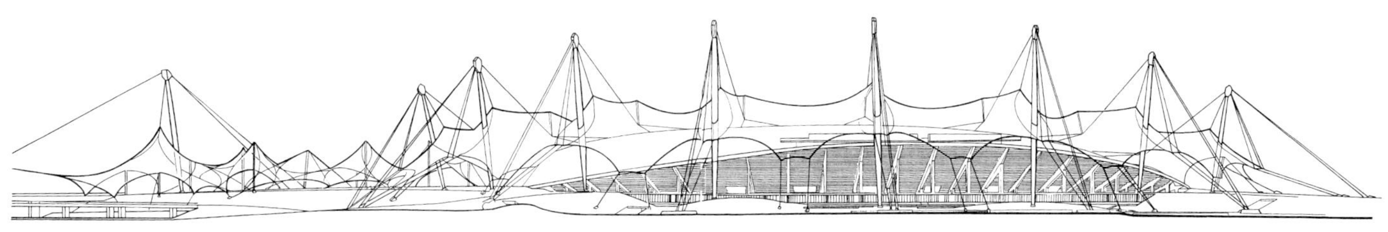

Santiago Calatrava
1951 Valencia

Santiago Calatrava ist ein Multitalent mit einer neuen ästhetischen Sprache. Er demonstriert damit zugleich die Rückkehr zum Handwerklich-Ingenieurhaften. Eine auffallende Homogenität des Gesamteindruckes, sozusagen eine übergeordnete ästhetische Gestalt, bestimmt sein eindrucksvolles Schaffen. Leider hat die Basler Bevölkerung eines seiner kühnsten Werke, eine Brücke über den Rhein, in einer Urabstimmung 1989 abgelehnt. Sein überaus facettenreiches Œuvre als Künstler-Architekt-Ingenieur wurde 1996 in einer Gesamtausstellung in Padua gezeigt. In einem Zürcher Patrizierhaus beim See sind Büros und Wohnung untergebracht. Mit seiner Frau Robertina spricht der Spanier auch schwedisch, mit den Kindern Schweizerdeutsch. Er denkt mit dem Stift; alles, was auf das Papier kommt, weist auf seine große Begabung als Künstler hin.

Santiago Calatrava
1951 Valencia

Santiago Calatrava is a man of many talents and a new aesthetic language, with which he also demonstrates a return to a technical/engineering ethic. A conspicuous homogeneity in the overall impression, a higher aesthetic form, so to speak, informs his impressive work. Unfortunately, one of his boldest works, a bridge over the Rhine, was rejected by the people of Basel in a referendum in 1989. His extremely multifaceted oeuvre as artist/architect/engineer was shown in 1996 in a comprehensive exhibition in Padua. A large patrician house by the lake in Zurich accommodates both offices and living space. Born Spanish, he also speaks Swedish with his wife Robertina and Schweizerdeutsch with the children. He thinks with his pencil; everything he sets down on paper shows his great talent as an artist.

Santiago Calatrava

Kunst ist Bau
Bau ist Kunst

Eduardo Chillida
1924 San Sebastian

Am äußersten Zipfel von San Sebastian am Golf von Biscaya stehen im Meer drei Eisenskulpturen «Peines del viento» von Eduardo Chillida, 1977 umrahmt von der Platzgestaltung, einer Gemeinschaftsarbeit mit Luis Peña Ganchegui. Dorthin hat Chillida meine Freunde und mich 1988 zu einem Rendezvous eingeladen. Im Kontext mit der bestehenden Architektur, einer auf ein Minimum ausgerichteten Plattform, und der umgebenden Meer-Natur werden seine Skulpturen sofort verständlich. Der Dreiklang von Natur, Urform und Landschaftsgestaltung war gewaltig. Dann ging es zurück ins Haus am Hang, dem Golf zugewandt, und von dort nach Donustia, zu seinem Atelier in der Landschaft. Später, 1990, gastierte er an einem Symposium der Basler Architektur-Vorträge in der Kunsthalle. Der sympathische Mann, dem Beziehungen wichtig sind, ist bei Gesprächen stets mit aller Offenheit zugegen.

76 *Eduardo Chillida Atelierhaus in Donustia (San Sebastian)*   *Eduardo Chillida's workshop in Donustia (San Sebastian)*

Eduardo Chillida
1924 San Sebastian

At the outermost tip of San Sebastian on the Bay of Biscay, three iron sculptures, "Peines del viento" (wind-combs) by Eduardo Chillida stand in the sea, framed in 1977 by the layout of the location, a joint project with Luis Peña Ganchegui. It was there that he invited my friends and me to a rendezvous in 1988. In the context of the existing architecture, a platform reduced to a minimum, and the surrounding seascape, his sculptures immediately make sense. The triad of nature, primal form and landscape was overpowering. We then went back to the house on the hill overlooking the Bay, and from there to Donustia, to his workshop in the landscape. Later, in 1990, he was a guest speaker at a symposium of the Basel Architektur Vorträge in the Kunsthalle. This likeable man, to whom relationships are important, is always completely open in discussions.

Jacques Herzog
1950 Basel

Askese des Materiellen wurde zu einem Haupt-Motiv seines architektonischen Œuvres. Jacques Herzogs Versuche, seine architektonische Welt mit minimalen Gestaltmitteln zu bestimmen, sind längst noch nicht an ihr schöpferisches Ende gelangt. Das erweist sich etwa an den Bearbeitungen der Kupferhülle an SBB-Stellwerken. Selten zuvor hat ein Basler Kollege sein Selbstverständnis als Architekt so ideenreich und überzeugend zu kommunizieren verstanden. Seine Passion zum Fußballspiel ist nicht zuletzt ein Zeichen dafür, daß er auch dem Volk nahestehen möchte. So ist seine selbstbewußte Architektur gut lesbar und stellt sich kraftvoll dar.

78 *Kupferhülle um das SBB-Stellwerk an der Münchensteinerbrücke in Basel, 1999*   *Copper cladding around the SBB signal box at the Münchensteinerbrücke in Basel, 1999*

Jacques Herzog
1950 Basel

Asceticism with regard to materials has become a main motif in his architectural oeuvre. Jacques Herzog's attempts to define his architectural world using the minimum of materials have by no means yet reached their creative conclusion. This is shown, for instance, by his treatments of the copper cladding on SBB signal boxes. Rarely before has a Basel colleague had the facility of communicating his or her self-conception so convincingly and with such a wealth of ideas. His passion for football is not least a sign that he feels close to the people. His confident architecture is thus well readable and powerfully presented.

Pierre de Meuron
1950 Basel

Pierre de Meuron und Jacques Herzog haben seit ihrer Gymnasialzeit den gleichen Bildungsweg einge-
schlagen. Auch ihre Gestaltsprache besitzt einen erstaunlichen Gemeinschaftscharakter. Im Jahre 1976
konnte ich mich von der Intelligenz Pierre de Meurons als Mitarbeiter in meinem Büro beim Wettbewerb
«Erneuerung Amtshaus Bern» überzeugen; er entwickelte mit Konsequenz ein einheitliches Gesamter-
scheinungsbild. Diese beiden Basler Pioniere zeigen eine Vielfalt im Formalen und Stilistischen, die den
Vergleich zur Meisterarchitektur ziehen läßt. Jedes ihrer Projekte strahlt seine eigenwillige Grundidee
aus. Das vorbildlich sanft restaurierte Haus Schaeffer, von Paul Artaria und Hans Schmidt 1928 in Riehen
gebaut, ist heute das Domizil der Familie de Meuron.

Um- und Neubau SUVA-Gebäude in Basel, 1993 – 94,
Broschüre zur Swissbau 99 «Vom Mass zum Messbaren»

Conversion and restoration of the SUVA building in Basel, 1993 – 94,
brochure for Swissbau 99 "Vom Mass zum Messbaren"

Pierre de Meuron
1950 Basel

Pierre de Meuron and Jacques Herzog have followed the same educational course since their grammar
school days. Even their formal language has an astonishingly concerted character. In 1976 I was able to
convince myself of Pierre de Meuron's intelligence when he worked in my offices on the competition for the
restoration of the Amtshaus in Bern; he developed a unified overall appearance with logical consistency.
These two Basel pioneers show a diversity of form and style which bears comparison with the architecture
of the masters. Each of their projects radiates its own individual basic concept. Haus Schaeffer, built in
Riehen by Paul Artaria and Hans Schmidt in 1928 and restored with exemplary sensitivity, is today the
home of the de Meuron family.

vom **Mass** zum **Messbaren**

Massstäbe und Proportionen
am Beispiel der Architektur

Eine Ausstellung der Tschudin AG
nach einem Konzept von Christian W. Blaser

Richard Lohse
1902 Zürich – 1988 Zürich

Jeder junge schöpferische Mensch sucht wohl gelegentlich Meister-Persönlichkeiten, um seine eigene Welt danach auszurichten. Nach meiner Rückkehr aus Chicago und Kyoto eröffnete mir Richard Lohse in seiner Position als Chefredaktor von «Bauen & Wohnen» eine Möglichkeit zur Publikation meines eigenen Mies van der Rohe-Foto- und Textmaterials. Dieser Einstieg verschaffte mir viel Goodwill. Bei der Planung meines Buches «Tempel und Teehaus in Japan» empfahl Lohse mir, das Layout so zu konzipieren, daß ein gleichsam virtuell mit einer Nadel durchgezogenes Loch ausnahmslos auf jeder Seite mit dem Satzspiegel harmonieren würde. Eine solcher Art verstandene «mise-en-page» ist ein Hand-Werk, das Mit-dem-Kopf-denken-und-mit-der-Hand-Tun. Bestimmt hat Lohse dies in seinen seriellen Bildern umsetzen können. Seine kulturelle Autorität zeigte, wie man den Sinn einer Gestalt in Geist umsetzt.

«Temples et Jardins au Japon» Werner Blaser, typographische Mithilfe: Richard Lohse, 1956

"Temples et Jardins au Japon" Werner Blaser, typographical assistance: Richard Lohse, 1956

Richard Lohse
1902 Zurich – 1988 Zurich

Every young creative person looks for master figures by whom he or she can orientate their own world. After my return from Chicago and Kyoto, Richard Lohse, in his position as editor in chief of "Bauen & Wohnen", gave me the opportunity to publish my own Mies van der Rohe photos and texts. This debut earned me a lot of goodwill. In planning my book "The temple and teahouse in Japan", Lohse advised me to conceive the layout in such a way that if an imaginary needle were to pierce a hole it would without exception harmonise with the printing area on each page. A *mise-en-page* understood in such a way is a craft, the craft of thinking with the head and acting with the hands. Lohse certainly must have employed this in his serial pictures. His cultural authority showed how the sense of a form is transformed into spirit.

Temples et Jardins au Japon

Norman Foster
1935 Manchester

Die Skizze, wie sie Norman Foster beherrscht, ist ein natürlicher Gegenpol zur digitalisierten Technologie. Dennoch brauchen die großen Architektur-Projekte die Computer-Anlagen für eine effiziente Entwicklung. Daher mißt das Skizzieren – das über seine kulturellen Wurzeln hinaus eine geistige Doktrin bei der Entwicklung eines Bauwerkes einnimmt – den Dingen einen um so höheren ästhetischen Wert zu. Den weltoffenen Briten Norman Foster – mit einem leidenschaftlichen Hang zum Aerodynamischen – beleben sein Schaffen ebenso sehr wie seine Passion zum Konstruieren. Mit ihm fanden Begegnungen in seinem Büro in London oder in seinem früheren Landhaus, sowie in meinem Büro in Basel statt. Seine Versuche, an ihr Ende gelangt.

Norman Foster
1935 Manchester

The drawing, as Norman Foster has mastered it, naturally forms an opposite pole to digitised technology. Nevertheless, big architectural projects require computer systems for efficient development. Drawing, which in addition to its cultural roots takes on the aspect of an intellectual doctrine in the development of a building, thus imbues things with an aesthetic value that is all the higher. The open-minded Briton with his enthusiastic inclination for aerodynamics is stimulated as much by his creative work as by his passion for construction. I met him in his office in London and at his former country house, as well as in my office in Basel. His attempts to define the representational world of architecture with the minimum of materials have by no means reached their conclusion as yet.

Roger Diener
1950 Basel

Das Werk von Roger Diener hat sich fernab von allen Trends mit äußerster Konsequenz entwickelt und
eine Tiefgründigkeit erreicht, die er mit moderner Auffassung in Einklang zu bringen weiß. Behutsam
reflektierend hat er ein Œuvre geschaffen und weiter gepflegt, dessen Ausstrahlung in der Basler Schule
der Architekten eine zentrale Rolle spielt. Seine oft imposanten Gebäude sind durch eine fragile Materialität
bestimmt. Deren städtebauliche Dimensionen, die als Zeile und Block zu identifizieren sind, haben im
In- und Ausland große Beachtung gefunden. Als Berufs-Kollege ist Roger Diener stets offen und zugäng-
lich. Seine Bereitschaft zum Mitmachen, sein intellektueller Enthusiasmus, im Kulturellen wie auch im
Alltäglichen, ist bemerkenswert und zeichnet sich durch einen ganz persönlichen Stil aus.

86 *Zoologischer Garten Basel, Flamingosteg, 1996*   *Basel Zoo, Flamingosteps, 1996*

Roger Diener
1950 Basel

Roger Diener's work has developed with the utmost logical consistency that is far removed from all
trends, and has attained a profundity that he harmonises with modern conceptualisation. With careful
reflection he has created and maintained an oeuvre whose charisma plays a central role among architects
of the Basel school. His often imposing buildings are defined by a fragile materiality. Their urbanistic
dimensions, identified as line and block, have awakened great interest at home and abroad. As a professional colleague, Roger Diener is always open and accessible. His readiness to participate, his intellectual
enthusiasm in cultural matters and in everyday life are remarkable and distinguished by a very personal
style.

Nicholas Grimshaw
1939 Hove (GB)

Gerne haftet man den Engländern das «Meccano» an: Architektur als Spiel, wie ein zerlegbares Puzzle, das auf einer begreifbaren Ordnung aufgebaut ist. Rühmenswert ist Nicholas Grimshaws Idee, mit Standardelementen eine Architektur aufzubauen. Stahl und Glas prägen zweifellos das Gesicht seiner Bauwerke. Seine Bauten aus vorgefertigten Einzelteilen sind bemerkenswerte Modulationen, und sie regen zu intensiver und differenzierter Betrachtung an. Nicholas Grimshaw steht in einer glanzvollen Tradition englischer Vornehmheit. Ob an einer Tagung in Weil am Rhein oder an der Swissbau 99, bei seinen Vorträgen tritt er immer ganz selbstverständlich als Gentleman auf. Seine Pointen kommen überzeugend wortmächtig daher.

88   *Waterloo International Terminal in London für die Eurostar-Züge, 1988–93*   *Waterloo International Terminal in London for the Eurostar trains, 1988–93*

Nicholas Grimshaw
1939 Hove (GB)

The English often have the "Meccano" label attached to them: architecture as a game, like a dismountable puzzle built on a comprehensible order. Nicholas Grimshaw's idea of constructing an architecture from standard elements is laudable. Steel and glass are undoubtedly the most characteristic features of his constructions. His buildings made of prefabricated units are remarkable modulations, and they inspire intensive and discriminating observation. Nicholas Grimshaw is part of an illustrious tradition of English distinction. Whether at a conference in Weil am Rhein or at the Swissbau 99, at his lectures he always appears quite naturally a gentleman. The points he makes are conveyed with convincing verbal power.

Zaha Hadid
1950 Bagdad

Fast jeder aufgeschlossene Architekt besitzt im Bücherregal das Traktat von Zaha Hadid. Die in London lebende Irakerin steigt in allen Teilen der Welt, Issey Miyake gekleidet, auf das Podium und trägt ihre Thesen in leidenschaftlicher Überzeugung vor, mittels Diagrammzeichnungen, die nicht immer die Wirklichkeit meinen, sondern eine Art Autonomie gegenüber der Wirklichkeit. Eine Frau, die der Männerwelt der Architekten die Stirn bieten kann. Sie rangiert vielfach in großen Wettbewerben obenauf und ist bei der jungen Architektengeneration sehr gefragt. Ihre Pavillons in Weil am Rhein sind von ihrer Grundlage her neu erfunden und eine Revolution des räumlichen Sehens und Denkens. Meine Gespräche mit ihr in Basel und Berlin bestärkten unsere These, daß das spontane Architekturerlebnis in Dauer und Kontinuität überzugehen hat. Dies bestätigt auch ihr eigenwilliges zeichnerisches Œuvre.

Landesgartenschau "Grün 99" in Weil am Rhein, Hadid's Pavilion LF one

Zaha Hadid
1950 Baghdad

Almost every open-minded architect has Zaha Hadid's treatise on his or her bookshelf. The London-based Iraqi mounts podiums all over the world, dressed by Issey Miyake, and presents her theses with passionate conviction by means of diagrams that are not always intended as reality, more a kind of autonomy with respect to reality. A woman who can hold her own in the male-dominated world of architects, she frequently ranks at the top in big competitions and is in great demand with the younger generation. Her pavilions in Weil am Rhein are fundamentally new inventions and a revolution in spatial vision and thinking. My talks with her in Basel and Berlin strengthened our thesis that the spontaneous architectural experience must pass over into permanence and continuity. This is also confirmed by her individualistic body of drawings.

Livio Vacchini
1933 Locarno

Ein neuer künstlerischer Wahrheitsgehalt ist im Werk von Livio Vacchini sichtbar geworden. Bei ihm werden «Streit» und Widerspruch nicht verdrängt, sondern bewußt in seine Arbeit inkorporiert. Man kann darum von einer Architektur im Übergang sprechen, d.h. einer Phase des Umbruchs, wo Tradiertes gründlich in Frage gestellt und dennoch über Traditionen etwas Andersgeartetes mit hohem Realitätsbezug entwickelt wird. Archetypische Bauwerke mit vorausweisendem Gestaltkanon. Seine Kritik am permanenten Architekturprojekt öffnet den Wahrheitsgehalt, was Architektur mit Gestalt sein kann. Sein erhebliches Maß an Kreativität bereicherte unsere persönliche Beziehung. Wir trafen anläßich seiner Vorträge in Wien, Zürich, Basel zusammen sowie in Locarno bei seiner gleichermaßen stillen wie konzentrierten Architekturarbeit – und den um so fröhlicheren Festen im Kreise seiner Tessiner Kollegen.

92 *Bucheinband «Livio Vacchini» von Werner Blaser, 1994*   *Book cover "Livio Vacchini" by Werner Blaser, 1994*

Livio Vacchini
1933 Locarno

A new artistic truth has become visible in the work of Livio Vacchini. Far from suppressing "quarrel" and contradiction, he consciously incorporates it into his work. It could thus be described as architecture in transition, or a phase of upheaval, where traditional values are fundamentally called into question and yet where the use of traditions develops something of a different nature with a strong relation to reality. Archetypal buildings with a forward-looking design canon. His criticism of the permanent architectural project opens up the truth of what architectural form can be. The considerable creativity in him has enriched our personal relationship. We met at his lectures in Vienna, Zurich and Basel, and in Locarno during his architectural work, both quiet and concentrated – and the parties, all the more joyful in comparison, with his colleagues from Ticino.

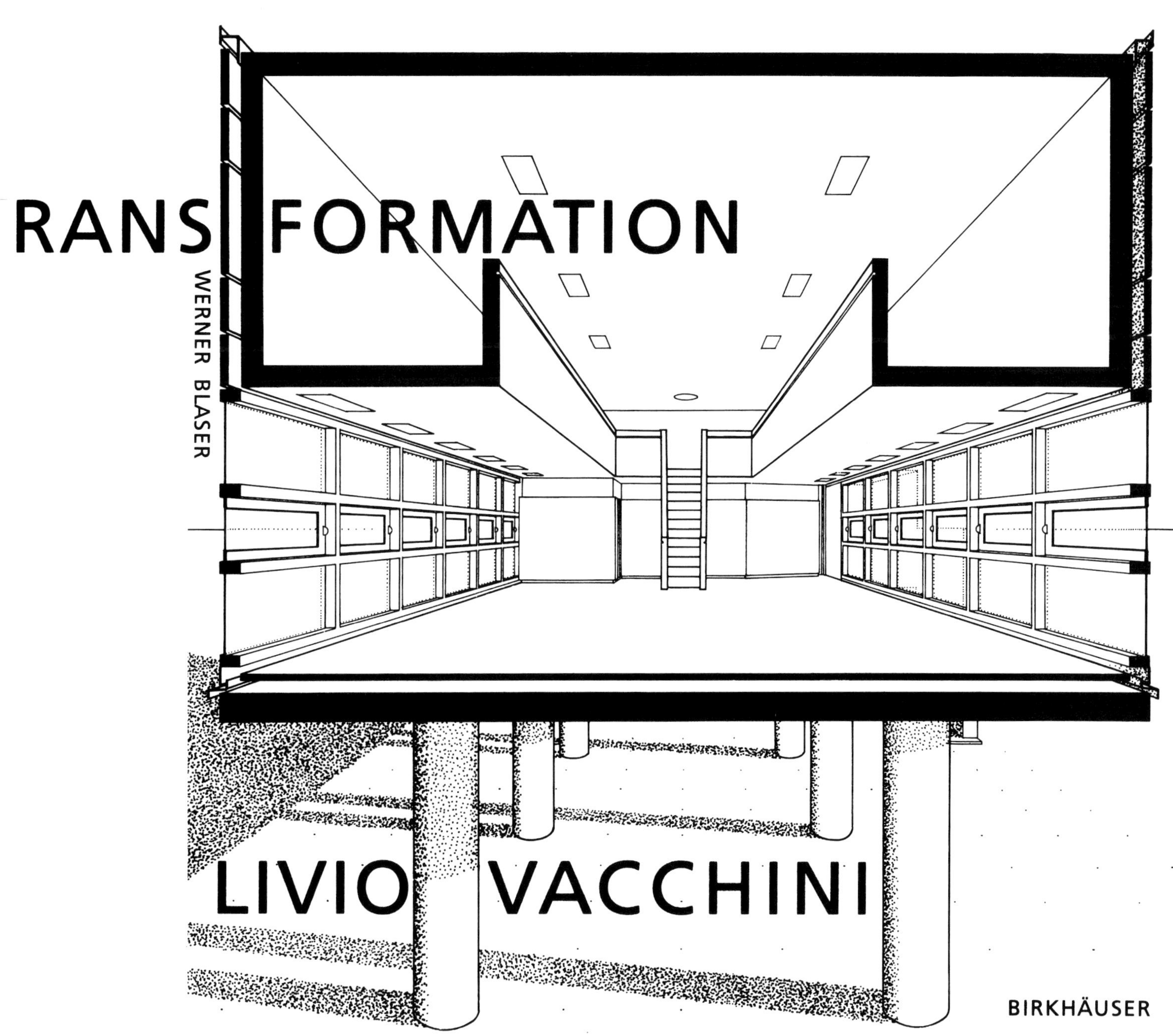
RANS FORMATION
WERNER BLASER
LIVIO VACCHINI
BIRKHÄUSER

Theo Hotz
1928 Oberrieden (Zürich)

Theo Hotz versteht die Architektur allein aus den Determinierungen von Material, Konstruktion und Technik. Im Spannungsfeld dieser Kräfte sind seine Gebäude mit ihrer Eigenart und Reinheit zu orten. Die Konstruktion bestimmt, analog zur Methodik des Industrial Design, die Erscheinungsform der Architektur. Die Subtilität des konstruktiven Denkens führt ihn von der angewandten zur freien Kunst. Es scheint also, daß er so verstanden werden muß, daß das Konstrukt beim Bau als das primäre Prinzip und seine Kunstsammlung als das sekundäre Prinzip seinen schöpferischen Charakter auszeichnen. Gesprächig, humorvoll-ironisch, großzügig, genial ist er nach außen, Subtilität und Sensibilität zeichnen sein Innen aus. Es ist darum sehr gerechtfertigt, daß ihn die ETH Zürich 1999 mit der Würde des Dr. h.c. ausgezeichnet hat.

94   *Weishaupt Verwaltungs- und Schulungszentrum in Geroldswil (Zürich), 1997–99*   *Weishaupt Verwaltungs- und Schulungszentrum in Geroldswil (Zurich), 1997–99*

Theo Hotz
1928 Oberrieden (Zurich)

Theo Hotz's understanding of architecture is derived exclusively from the determinations of material, construction and technology. His buildings, with their individuality and purity, can be located in the force-field between these factors. Analogous to the methodology of industrial design, construction determines the appearance of architecture. The subtlety of constructional thought leads him from applied to free art. It seems he must be understood as having his creative character distinguished by the primary principle of the construct in building and the secondary principle of his art collection. He is outwardly talkative, humorously ironic, generous and brilliant, while inwardly he is subtle and sensitive. It is therefore more than justifiable that the ETH Zurich awarded him an honorary doctorate in 1999.

Richard Meier
1934 Newark (New Jersey)

Das Werk des Amerikaners Richard Meier ist eine wichtige Komponente der aktuellen Architektur-Ästhetik. Seine spezifische Konzeption von Schönheit, in der entscheidenden Ausprägung einer Architektur in allumfassendem Weiß, zeigt Schlichtheit und Selbstgenügsamkeit, die zugunsten innerer Werte auf äußeren Prunk verzichtet. Obwohl auch bei ihm die Computertechnologie das Bauwerk bestimmt, behält die weiße Farbe eine gleichsam moralische, beinahe metaphysische Dimension. In seinen beiden Büros in New York und Los Angeles, sowie bei vielen Begegnungen in Basel, Paris, Ulm, München und Washington war es für mich immer eine Bereicherung zu erleben, wie er seine künstlerisch-geistige Kreativität auch einer breiten Öffentlichkeit zu vermitteln versteht. Den ausgeprägten Charakter seiner Lebensart, so etwa pflegt er einen regen Umgang im Architekten- und Künstlermilieu, lernte ich seit 1986 in unzähligen Begegnungen schätzen.

 Weishaupt-Forum in Schwendi (Ulm), 1987–92   *Weishaupt-Forum in Schwendi (Ulm), 1987–92*

Richard Meier
1934 Newark (New Jersey)

The work of the American Richard Meier is an important component of the current architectural aesthetic. His specific conception of beauty, in its decisive form of an architecture in all-embracing white, shows a simplicity and modesty which dispenses with outer show in favour of inner values. Although computer technology determines his buildings as well, the colour white retains a sort of moral, almost metaphysical dimension. In his two offices in New York and Los Angeles, as well as in many meetings Basel, Paris, Ulm, Munich and Washington it was always enriching for me to experience his facility for conveying his artistic and intellectual creativity even to a more general public. I have come to appreciate the distinctive character of his lifestyle (he takes an active part in the architectural and artistic scene) in countless meetings since 1986.

Juhani Pallasmaa
1936 Finnland

Ein großer Denker und eine Autorität unter den finnischen Architekten ist Juhani Pallasmaa. Zweierlei Interessen beschäftigen ihn: einerseits die Analogien zur «Morphogenese» der Natur Lapplands, andererseits der innere Dialog zwischen Realismus und Moderne. Aus dieser Dialektik von Natur und Gegenwart geht bei ihm eine befreiende Wirkung aus. Noch eine Eigenschaft zeichnet ihn aus, die des loyalen Botschafters der finnischen Architekten in der weiten Welt. Und so trafen wir uns in Helsinki und Basel, immer herrschte in seinen Gesprächen eine sinnliche Präsenz von Dingen und Orten, Natur und Architektur. Sein Thema bei seinem Basler Architektur Vortrag «The Eyes of the Skin» könnte kaum klarer gefaßt werden als im Vergleich, daß in einem Ast der Bauplan des Baumes verankert ist. Pallasmaa leistete eine wesentliche Mitarbeit bei den Büchern «Animal Architecture» und «The Language of Wood».

 Aus dem Buch: «The Melnikov House» von Juhani Pallasmaa, 1996   *From the book "The Melnikov House" by Juhani Pallasmaa, 1996*

Juhani Pallasmaa
1936 Finland

Juhani Pallasmaa is one of the great thinkers and authorities among Finnish architects. He has two interests: analogies to the "morphogenesis" of nature in Lapland, and the inner dialogue between realism and modernity. This dialectic between nature and the present produces a liberating effect for him. He has another distinguishing role, that of loyal ambassador for Finnish architects in the world at large. When we met in Helsinki and Basel there was always a tangible presence of things and places, nature and architecture in the things he said. The theme of his architectural lecture "The Eyes of the Skin" in Basel is nowhere better summarised than in the simile that one branch holds the blueprint for the tree. Pallasmaa has made a considerable contribution to the books "Animal Architecture" and "The Language of Wood".

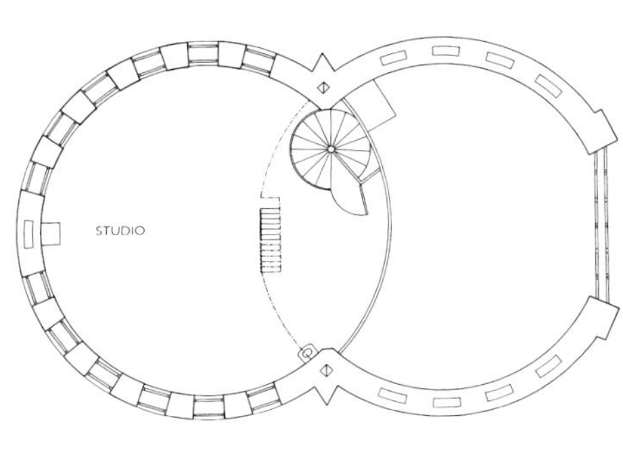

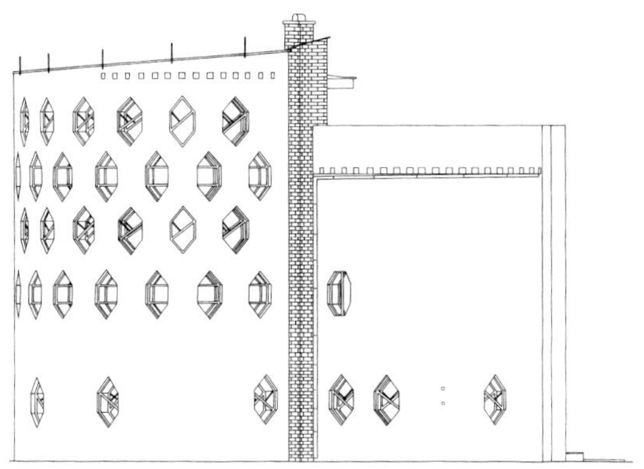

ABOVE: Second floor plan; BELOW: Side elevation

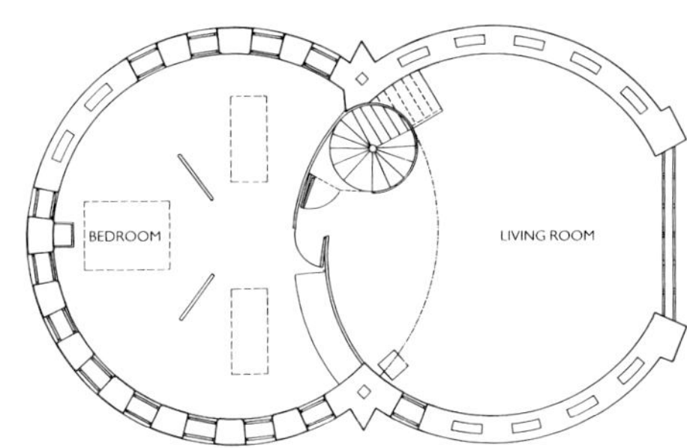

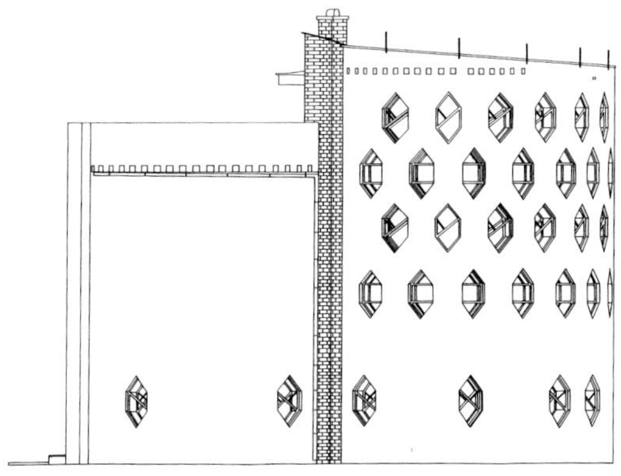

ABOVE: First floor plan; BELOW: Side elevation

Renzo Piano
1937 Genua

Man kann die Bauten Renzo Pianos in einem weit umfassenderen Sinn denn bei anderen Architekten als topogen bezeichnen, als von einem bestimmten Ort ausgehend. Ein weiteres Prinzip ist die Suche nach der Wahrheit des Konstrukts. Die Korrespondenz zwischen Aufgabe und Verwirklichung, zwischen Detail und Ganzem führt zu einer überaus feinnervigen Architektur von höchstem Einklang. Damit schafft Piano eine Grundstimmung, die auch immer wieder in der persönlichen Begegnung den Ton angibt. Vor dem Bauherrn erscheint er immer mit zwei Mitarbeitern. Beim Bau des Beyeler Museums etwa mit dem Projektchef vom Büro in Paris Bernard Plattner und Loïc Couton. Der kreative Prozeß wird damit ganz im Sinne der Auseinandersetzung mittels seiner Skizzen durchgezogen. In seiner Tischrede im Weißen Haus 1998 sagte er: «Ich habe meinen Vater schon früh zu den Baustellen begleitet, war fasziniert davon, Dinge aus dem Nichts, allein durch die Hand des Menschen entstehen zu sehen.»

100

Museum Beyeler in Riehen (Basel), 1991 – 97; Foto: Christo wrapped trees, November 1998

Beyeler Museum in Riehen (Basel), 1991 – 97; Photo: Christo wrapped trees, November 1998

Renzo Piano
1937 Genoa

Renzo Piano's buildings can be described as topogenous, as being of a specific place, in a far more comprehensive sense than is the case with other architects. A further principle is the search for the truth of a construct. The correspondence between task and realisation, between detail and whole leads to an extremely sensitive architecture of great harmony. Piano thereby creates a basic atmosphere that also sets the tone in every personal meeting. When he meets a building sponsor he will always bring two of his staff with him. For the Beyeler Museum, for instance, he brought the project chief from the Paris office, Bernard Plattner, and Loïc Couton. The creative process is thus carried out wholly in the spirit of a debate on the basis of his drawings. In his after-dinner speech at the White House in 1998 he said: "I went with my father to building sites from an early age. I was fascinated by seeing things being created out of nothing simply through the actions of people".

Arthur Rüegg
1942 Zürich

Arthur Rüegg, Professor an der Architekturabteilung der ETH Zürich, war der Regisseur eines Buches über meine Möbel, welches von Katharina Steib vermittelt und durch Charles von Büren textlich begleitet wurde. Der erstgenannte war bei diesem Projekt mit intellektueller Wahrheit und kritischer Neugierde mit dabei. Im Buch war sein persönliches Engagement klar umrissen und wurde zum integrierenden Bestandteil meiner Selbstdarstellung. Arthur Ruegg ist auch ein bekannter Le Corbusier-Forscher; so hat er etwa dessen «Polychromie architecturale» kritisch ediert, und er arbeitet an einem fundamentalen Werk über das Möbel-Design des Meisters. Und dann ist er noch ein Sammler von allem, was konstruktive Logik beinhaltet. So besitzt er z.B. ein Fotobild von mir: ein Porträtfoto von Mies in seiner Wohnung in Chicago von 1964 und einer Innenaufnahme seines Barcard-Gebäudes in Mexico-City, letzteres auf dem Kopf stehend, da ich den Film zweimal einspannte.

Arthur Rüegg
1942 Zurich

Arthur Rüegg, a professor in the Architectural Department at the ETH in Zurich, was the producer of a book about my furniture, which was arranged by Katharina Steib and had an accompanying text by Charles von Büren. Rüegg participated in the project with intellectual accuracy and critical curiosity. His personal commitment in the book was clearly defined and became an integrating component in my self-portrait. Arthur Rüegg is also a well-known Le Corbusier researcher; he has critically edited "Polychromie architecturale", and is preparing a fundamental work on the master's furniture design. He is also a collector of anything that involves constructive logic. He has, for example, a photograph of mine: a portrait of Mies in his apartment in Chicago in 1964 and an interior shot of his Barcard building in Mexico City, the latter standing on its head, as I wound the film in twice.

Verbinden
Fugen
Joint
Connection
Werner Blaser

Stefan Polónyi
1930 Gyula (Ungarn)

Der Ingenieur Stefan Polónyi lebt und arbeitet in Köln. Bei ihm haben Harmonie und Schönheit ebensoviel Gewicht wie Konstruktion und Funktion. Nur wenige Ingenieure haben gelernt, von Statik zur Dynamik, von Struktur zur Gestalt umzudenken. Wir sollten uns darauf besinnen, daß Architektur «Bau-Kunst» ist und die Ingenieur-Disziplin «Ingenieur-Kunst» heißt; beide sollten im Dienste einer lebenswert gestalteten Umwelt stehen. Ich erinnere mich an das Treffen zu den Architektur Vorträgen in Basel, wo Polónyi sein statisches Werk der DB-Bahnhofhallen-Erweiterung in Köln gleichermaßen brillant strukturierte und visualisierte. Ihre endgültige Entschlüsselung bleibt freilich dem aufmerksam betrachtenden Bahnfahrer vorbehalten. Kunst ist Bau ist Kunst, könnte man darum sagen.

104 *Erneuerung der Vordächer am Hauptbahnhof in Köln, 1985–91*   *Renovation of the canopies at Cologne main station, 1985–91*

Stefan Polónyi
1930 Gyula (Hungary)

The engineer Stefan Polónyi lives and works in Cologne. Harmony and beauty carry as much weight for him as construction and function. Only a few engineers have learned to rethink from statics to dynamics, from structure to form. We should remember that architecture is the "art of building" and that the engineering discipline means the "art of engineering"; both of them should be at the service of an environment that is appropriate to a life worth living. I remember the meeting at the Architektur Vorträge in Basel where Polónyi structured and visualised with equal brilliance his static work on the DB station extension in Cologne. Its final decoding is of course the preserve of the attentive rail traveller. Art is building is art, one could say.

Richard Horden
1944 Leominster (England)

Ein treuer Freund ist Richard Horden aus London. Es reizt ihn, das Britische und das Schweizerische, den Queen's Stand und das Skihaus in Vorträgen spannungsvoll gegenüberzustellen. Er findet damit einen Austausch zwischen Groß und Klein, zwischen Makrokosmos und Mikrokosmos. Großzügige Konzeption und detaillierte Durcharbeitung sind kennzeichned für seine Werke. Im «Light Tech», wie ich seine Architektur nenne, sind zweierlei Begriffe enthalten: Licht und Leicht. Gerade «Light Tech» wurde bei Horden zum gewinnenden Dialog – «touch the earth lightly» – zwischen Realismus und Abstraktion. Der Hang zum Pädagogischen hat ihn an die Technische Universität nach München und als Visiting-Professor an Architekturschulen in der ganzen Welt geführt. In Basel war er Gast bei den Basler Architekturvorträgen.

106 *Zeichnung «SkiHaus», 1991*   *Drawing of the "SkiHaus", 1991*

Richard Horden
1944 Leominster (England)

Richard Horden from London is a true friend. He delights in making stimulating comparisons in lectures between the British and the Swiss, the Queen's Stand and the Skihaus. He finds an interchange in this between large and small, between macrocosm and microcosm. Generous conception and detailed execution are the hallmarks of his work. "Light Tech", as I call his architecture, encompasses the concept of light in both its senses. It was "Light Tech" that became a winning dialogue – "touch the earth lightly" – between realism and abstraction. His inclination for teaching has led him to the Technische Universität in Munich and as visiting professor to architecture schools all over the world. In Basel he was a guest at the Basel Architektur Vorträge.

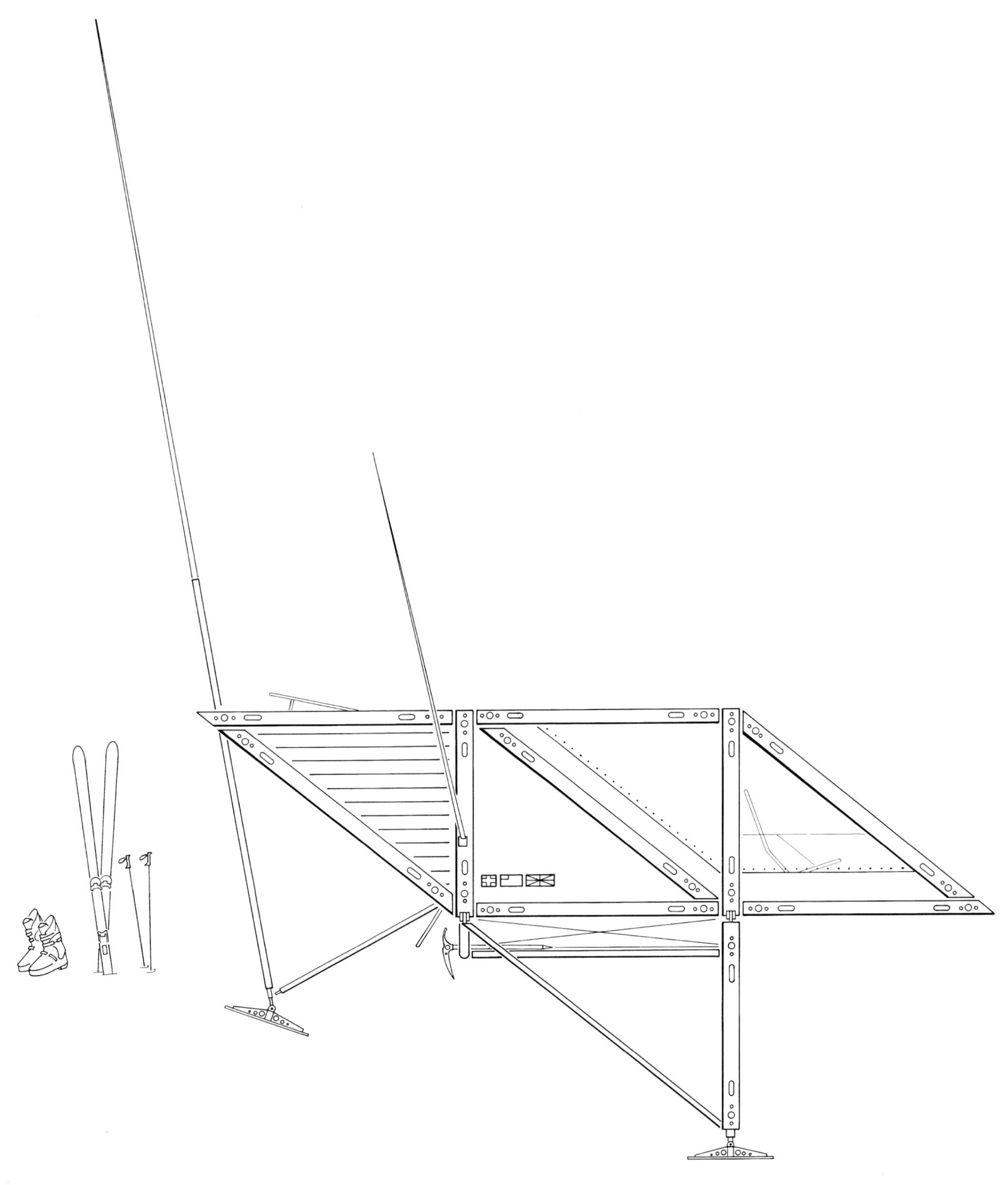

Werner Sobek
1953 Aalen (Württemberg)

Das scharf gezeichnete Œuvre von Werner Sobek, auf einem seriösen «Engineering» entwickelt, hat nun die Welt der modernen Architekten erreicht. Er ist einer der wenigen, die in der Lage sind, die Ästhetik einer Konstruktion in Leichtigkeit umzusetzen. In unserer zwiespältigen Zeit hat er der Ingenieur-Kunst eine markante Identität verliehen. Seine Ökonomie, ja Askese des Materiellen sind die Wurzeln eines zarten, von Schönheit begleiteten strukturellen Gefüges. Es ist darum nicht verwunderlich, daß er als Pate im aktuellen Werk von Helmut Jahn auftritt. Und so haben wir drei uns zu motivierenden Gesprächen über «Archi-neering» in Chicago zusammengefunden. In der Strenge und Disziplin der Einzelelemente entsteht Durchsichtigkeit, in diesem Zusammenwirken wird ein Bauwerk wahr. Selten seit der Tätigkeit von Robert Maillart hat ein Bauingenieur so viel Ästhetisches in dieser Disziplin so realistisch zu entwickeln versucht.

108

BMW-Pavillon in Frankfurt 1995 – 97, aus «Werner Sobek, Ingenieur-Kunst» von Werner Blaser, 1999

BMW pavilion in Frankfurt 1995 – 97, from "Werner Sobek, Ingenieur-Kunst" by Werner Blaser, 1999

Werner Sobek
1953 Aalen (Württemberg)

Werner Sobek's sharply drawn oeuvre, developed on a serious engineering base, has now reached the world of modern architects. He is one of the few capable of translating the aesthetic of a construction into lightness. In our contradictory times, he has given a clear-cut identity to the art of engineering. His economy, even asceticism, with materials is at the root of a delicate structural fabric with an element of beauty. It is therefore unsurprising that he appears as godfather in Helmut Jahn's current work. And so the three of us met up for motivating discussions on "Archi-neering" in Chicago. The severity and discipline of the individual elements creates a transparency; this synergy produces a building. Seldom since the work of Robert Maillart has a construction engineer attempted to develop so much that is aesthetic in this discipline so realistically.

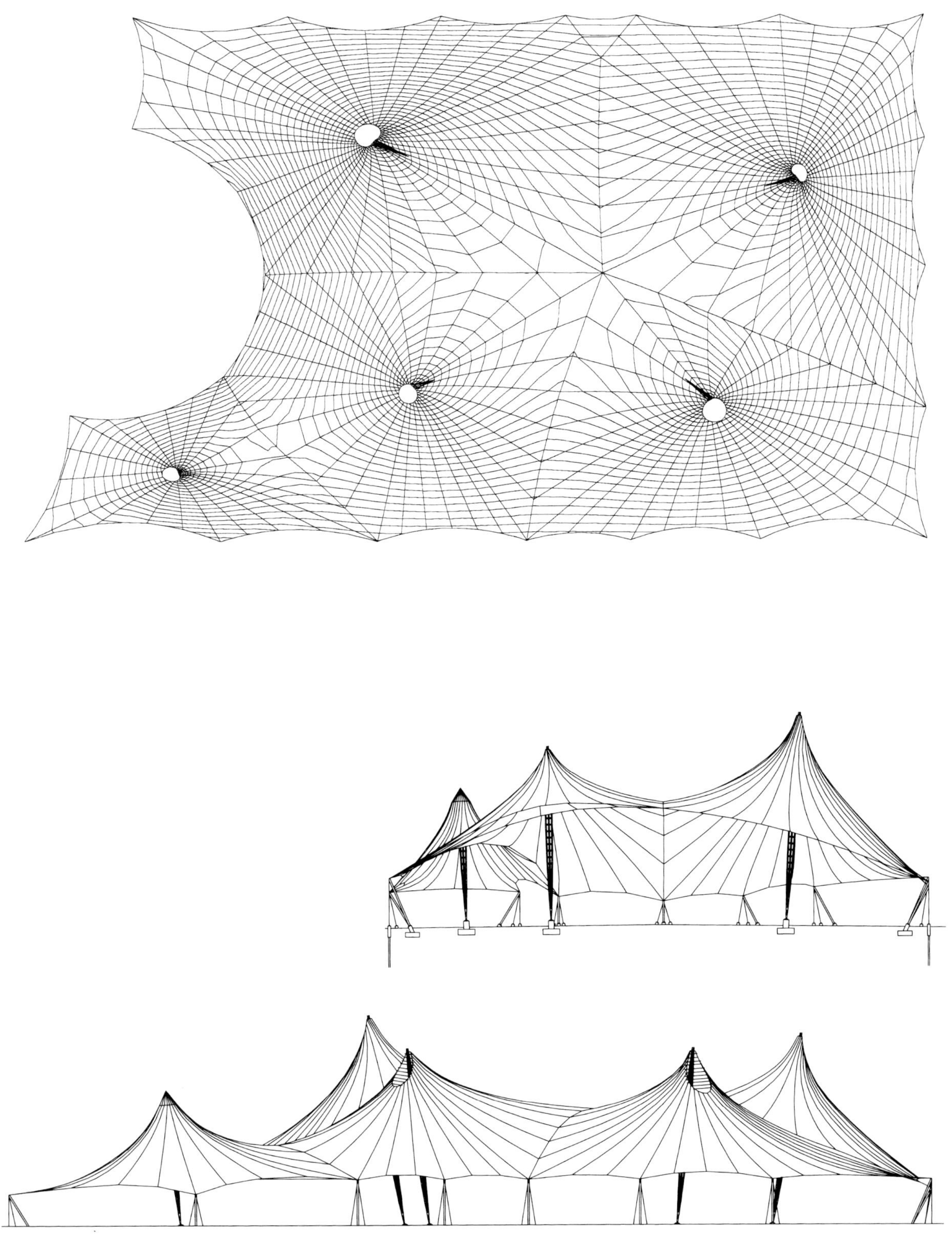

Hans Zaugg
1936 Derendingen

Seit bald zehn Jahren treffen mein Sohn Christian und ich Hans Zaugg etwa 4 Mal jährlich in seinem Atelier-
wohnhaus zu einem intensiven Gespräch. Als Miterfinder der «Swatch» ist ihm jedes Formgeschwätz
suspekt. Seine Thesen zu Markt und Management mögen für viele Industrielle eher geheimnisvoll, gar
unverständlich klingen; sie nehmen ihre Inspiration von einer Zurück-zu-den-Wurzeln-Idee. Dazu gründete
Hans Zaugg eine Schule für Gestaltung. Mit einer kleinen Gruppe von Studenten wird das Programm einer
industriellen Produktgestaltung umgekehrt und mit bekehrendem Wissen, das höher als alle Vernunft
ist, aber nicht gegen die Vernunft, wird das jeweilige Produkt entwickelt. Als kritischer Regionalist mit
Inhalten und Visionen machte ihn seine Integrität zu einer der geachtetsten Protagonisten der Gegenwart.

«Nomaa» (100'000-Franken-Haus), entwickelt im Zentrum für Innovation und Design, Derendingen, 1998

"Nomaa" (100'000-Franken-Haus), developed at the Zentrum für Innovation und Design, Derendingen, 1998

Hans Zaugg
1936 Derendingen

For almost ten years now, my son Christian and I have been meeting Hans Zaugg about four times a year
at his studio-cum-house for intensive discussion. As the joint inventor of the "Swatch", he does not take
kindly to polite chitchat. His theories on the market and management may seem somewhat obscure or
even incomprehensible to many industrialists; they take their inspiration from the idea of going back to the
roots, in pursuit of which Hans Zaugg founded a design school. With a small group of students, the pro-
gramme of industrial product design is stood on its head and with a prophetic knowledge that is higher
than any reason but not against reason, each of the products is developed. As a critical regionalist of
substance and vision, his integrity has made him one of the most respected protagonists of the present
day.

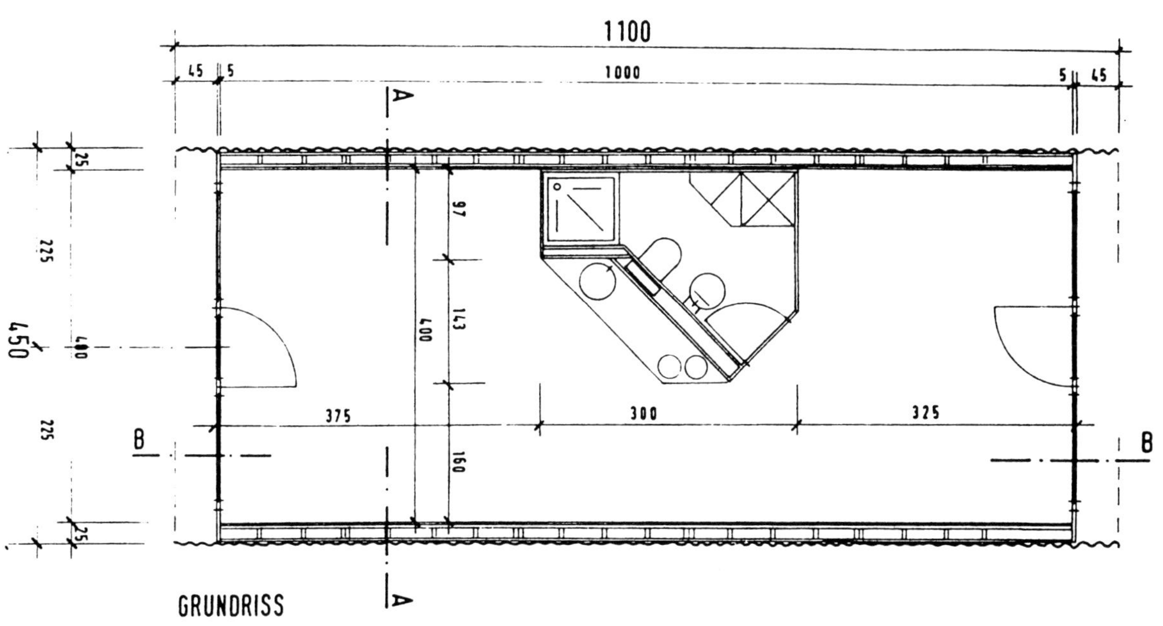

GRUNDRISS

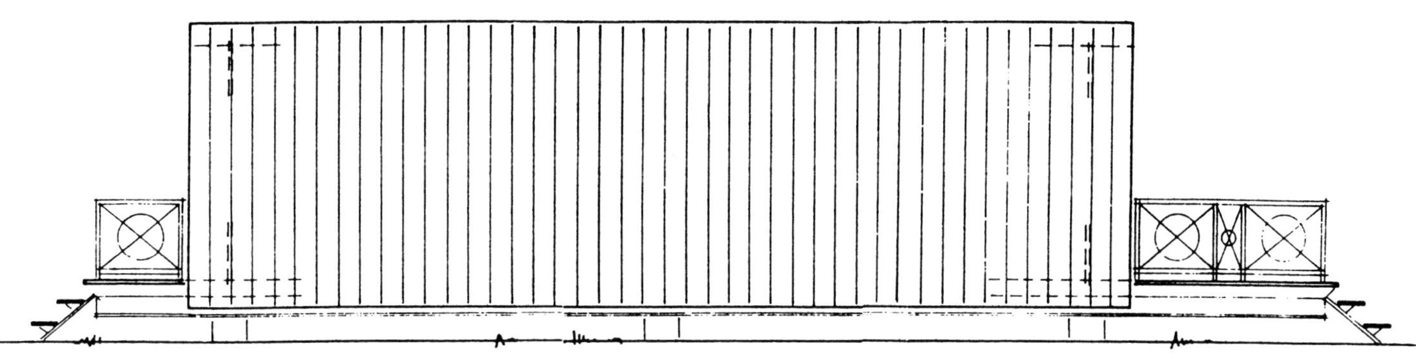

ANSICHT WEST UND OST

Peter Zumthor
1943 Basel

Wie der Schreibende entwickelte der im Kanton Baselland aufgewachsene und im bündnerischen Haldenstein lebende Peter Zumthor seinen eigentlichen Beruf auf der Grundlage einer handwerklichen Berufslehre. Von dieser Grundschulung her stammt die Vertiefung in das Material, um sich so in das Wesen der Dinge und der Aufgabe einzufühlen. Zunehmend entpuppte sich seine Architektur in ihrer Eigentümlichkeit, deren Gestalt mehr und mehr reduziert und komprimiert wurde. So hat er sich als konsequente und starke Persönlichkeit entwickelt, die ihn zu gestalterischer Verdichtung und Objektivierung zwang. Damals, kurz nach der Ausbildung an der Fachklasse für Innenausbau in Basel, kam er mit einem perfekten Portofolio in mein Atelier, um mich nach seinem Weitergehen zu befragen. Ich empfahl ihm Jean Prouvé in Paris; er wählte jedoch, um sich weiter zu schulen, das Pratt Institute in New York.

112 *Haus Gugelun bei Versam, 1990–93*   *Haus Gugelun near Versam, 1990–93*

Peter Zumthor
1943 Basel

Peter Zumthor grew up in the Canton of Baselland and lives in Haldenstein in Graubünden, and like the author, his actual profession developed from the basis of his apprenticeship as a craftsman. From this training comes the absorption in the material that allows him to feel his way into the essence of things and of the task. His architecture emerged as increasingly idiosyncratic, its form ever more reduced and compressed. Thus he has developed into a consistent and powerful personality, forced into creative condensation and objectivisation. Shortly after his training at the Fachklasse für Innenausbau in Basel, he came to my studio with a perfect portfolio to ask my advice about his further career. I recommended Jean Prouvé in Paris to him, but he wanted to train further and chose the Pratt Institute in New York.

Nachwort

Um die Architektur bewegen sich mehrere Disziplinen, von der Graphik zur Kunst und vom Design zur Statik. Architektur ist ein Bekenntnis zum Gesamtkunstwerk. Im Zusammenführen dieser gleichwertigen Disziplinen zu einem neuen kreativen Ausdruck entsteht eine Steigerung. Nach Laotse ist alles Lebendige dem Wechsel unterworfen. Es entfaltet sich und kehrt dann zum Ursprung zurück. So auch die Architektur, die entsteht, sich entwickelt und sich verändert. Ohne die weltweiten persönlichen Beziehungen würde Architektur zur leeren Geste.

Aber wie begegnen? Es verlangt Offenheit und Anpassung, Geben und Nehmen. Nachdenken und das Photo-Objektiv führen zur bewahrenden Vertiefung. So entsteht ein Gegenüber, das gepflegt werden muß, lange bevor es vermittelt werden kann. Während meiner ständigen Wanderschaft seit fünfzig Jahren wurden Beziehungen aufgebaut, im stetigen Dialog vermittelt und gepflegt, in gleichzeitiger Auseinandersetzung mit dem Erbe der Moderne. Insofern sie die Dimension eines kulturellen Selbstbewußtseins unserer Zeit reflektieren, sind diese fünfzig Begegnungen auch ein Zeugnis aktueller Baukultur. Das Niedergeschriebene und in Bildern Festgehaltene soll nicht zuletzt die junge Architektengeneration inspirieren und zur Selbstfindung animieren. Seit drei Jahren nutze ich das «professionelle» Podium der Swissbau Messe Basel für die Basler Architektur-Vorträge. Die Vorträge sind auf fünf Tage konzentriert

Afterword

Architecture involves several disciplines, from graphics to art and from design to statics. It is an affirmation of the integrated work of art. An intensification comes about, through the combination of several equally valuable disciplines into a new creative expression. According to Laotse, all living things are subject to change. They blossom and then return to their source. The same is true of architecture, which comes into being, develops and changes. Without worldwide personal relationships, architecture would become an empty gesture.

But how do we encounter one another? This requires openness and adaptation, giving and taking. Reflection and the camera lens preserve our encounters. An image is thus created, which needs to be cultivated long before it can be conveyed. My constant wanderings over fifty years, building up, cultivating and facilitating relationships are the dialogue, the coming to grips with the legacy of modernity. In so far as they reflect the aspect of a cultural self-confidence of our time, these fifty encounters are also a testament to contemporary architectural culture. What I have written down and captured in pictures is intended not least to inspire the younger generation of architects and encourage them to find themselves.

For three years now I have been using the "professional" platform of Basel's Swissbau fair for the Basel Architektur Vorträge. The lectures are concentrated into five days and reach a wide audience, far beyond

Basler
Architektur
Vorträge

und erreichen ein großes Publikum, weit über die Basler Grenzen hinaus. Die Basler Architektur-Vorträge genießen auf der einen Seite die finanzielle Unterstützung der Mitveranstalter, den Fachverbänden von Basel Stadt und Basel-Land und auf der andern Seite vom Sonderveranstaltungsbudget der Swissbau. Von der Messe Basel ist es Direktor Jürg Böhni und von der Swissbau Susanne Gysin, die mir in zuvorkommender Unterstützung Enthusiasmus und viel Positives ohne Wenn und Aber für diese Projekte entgegenbrachten. Ihnen gehört mein aufrichtiger Dank.

the bounds of Basel. The BAV thus enjoy the financial support both of their co-organisers, the professional associations of the city and province of Basel, and of Swissbau's special events budget. Director Jürg Böhni from the Messe Basel, and Susanne Gysin from Swissbau, in their courteous support, showed enthusiasm for these projects and a positivity that was unconditional. To them go my sincere thanks.

Architekten in alphabetischer Reihenfolge

Architects in alphabetical order

Alvar Aalto	16
Joseph Albers	50
Tadao Ando	68
Paul Artaria	14
Günter Behnisch	72
Max Bill	56
Aulis Blomstedt	18
Mario Botta	66
Jacques Brownson	24
Santiago Calatrava	74
Alfred Caldwell	54
Eduardo Chillida	76
Roger Diener	86
Charles Eames	64
Aldo van Eyck	20
Rolf Fehlbaum	40
Norman Foster	84
Karl Gerstner	42
Bertrand Goldberg	26
Myron Goldsmith	28
William Graatsma	44
Nicholas Grimshaw	88
Zaha Hadid	90
Jacques Herzog	78
Richard Horden	106
Theo Hotz	94
Helmut Jahn	46
Phyllis Lambert	48
Richard Lohse	82
Richard Meier	96
Pierre de Meuron	80
Ludwig Mies van der Rohe	22
Frei Otto	70
Juhani Pallasmaa	98

Ieoh Ming Pei	58
Renzo Piano	100
Stefan Polónyi	104
Gerrit Rietveld	60
Arthur Rüegg	102
Georg Schmidt	34
Otto Senn	38
Werner Sobek	108
Johannes Spalt	52
Gene Summers	30
Jean Tinguely	36
Livio Vacchini	92
Robert Venturi	62
Frank Lloyd Wright	32
Hans Zaugg	110
Peter Zumthor	112

Bücher von/Books by Werner Blaser

Tempel und Teehaus in Japan,
Urs Graf Verlag, Olten 1955
Temples et jardins au Japon,
Editions Albert Moranc, Paris 1956
Japanese Temples and Tea-Houses,
F.W. Dodge Corp., New York, 1956

Wohnen und Bauen in Japan/
Classical Dwelling Houses in Japan,
Verlag Arthur Niggli, Niederteufen, 1958

Struktur und Gestalt in Japan,
Verlag für Architektur, Zürich, 1963
Structure and Form in Japan,
Wittenborn & Co., New York, 1963

Mies van der Rohe –
Die Kunst der Struktur,
Verlag für Architektur, Zürich, 1965
Mies van der Rohe – L'Art de la Structure/
The Art of Structure,
Praeger Publishers, New York, 1965
Mies van der Rohe – El Arte de la Estructura,
Carlos Hirsch, Buenos Aires, 1965

Paperback: Mies van der Rohe
– Verlag für Architektur, Zürich, 1972
– Thames & Hudson, London, 1972
– Editorial Gustavo Gili, Barcelona, 1973
– A.D.A. Edita, Tokyo, 1976
– Zanichelli Editore, Bologna, 1977
– Uitgeverij Olo, Rotterdam, 1986

Objektive Architektur – Beispiel
«Skin and Skeleton»/
Objective Architecture – Example
«Skin and Skeleton»,
Richard Scherpe Verlag, Krefeld, 1970

Chinesische Pavillon-Architektur/
Chinese Pavillon Architecture,
Verlag Arthur Niggli, Niederteufen, 1974

Strukturale Architektur aus Osteuropa/
Structural Architecture of Eastern Europe
Zbinden Druck & Verlag, Basel, 1975

Der Fels ist mein Haus/
Le Roche est ma Demeure/
The Rock is my Home,
Wepf Verlag, Basel 1976

Struktur und Textur/
Structure and Texture,
Richard Scherpe Verlag, Krefeld, 1976

Prinzip einer Architektur –
Retrospektive 25 Jahre Werner Blaser,
Bündner Kunstmuseum, Chur 1977

Mies van der Rohe – Lehre und Schule/
Principles and School,
Birkhäuser Verlag, Basel, 1977
Mies van der Rohe – After Mies,
van Nostrand Reinhold Company,
New York, 1977
Mies van der Rohe – Continuing
The Chicago School of Architecture,
Birkhäuser Verlag, Basel, 1981,
second enlarged edition

Holz Haus/Maison de Bois/Wood Houses,
Wepf Verlag, Basel, 1980
2. erweiterte Auflage, 1985

Filigran Architektur/
Architecture en filigran/
Filigree Architecture,
Wepf Verlag, Basel, 1980

Courtyard House in China/
Hofhaus in China
Birkhäuser Verlag, Basel, 1979
Zweite Auflage/2nd edition 1995

Il design de Mies van der Rohe,
Electra Editrice, Milano, 1980
Mies van der Rohe – Furniture and Interiors,
Academy Editions, London, 1980
Mies van der Rohe – Les Maîtres du Design,
Electra Moniteur, Paris, 1980
Mies van der Rohe – Möbel und Interieurs,
Deutsche Verlagsanstalt, Stuttgart, 1981

Il design di Alvar Aalto,
Electa Editrice, Milano, 1981
Alvar Aalto als Designer,
Deutsche Verlagsanstalt, Stuttgart, 1982

Architecture 70/80 in Switzerland,
Birkhäuser Verlag, Basel, 1981
Textausgaben: in deutsch, en français,
in lingua italiana, en español,
versão portuguesa,
second enlarged edition, 1982
compendious presentation, 1983
(English, française, Español)

Klappstühle/Folding Chairs,
Birkhäuser Verlag, Basel, 1982

Elementare Bauformen/
Elemental Building Forms,
Beton Verlag, Düsseldorf, 1982

Schweizer Holzbrücken/
Ponts du Bois en Suisse/
Wooden Bridges in Switzerland,
Birkhäuser Verlag, Basel, 1982

Bauernhaus der Schweiz,
Birkhäuser Verlag, Basel, 1983

Drawings of Great Buildings/
Zeichnungen großer Bauten,
Birkhäuser Verlag, Basel, 1983

Architecture and Nature –
The Work of Alfred Caldwell/
Architecture et Nature –
L'Œuvre d'Alfred Caldwell/
Architektur und Natur –
das Werk von Alfred Caldwell,
Birkhäuser Verlag, Basel, 1984

Element – System – Möbel,
Deutsche Verlagsanstalt, Stuttgart, 1984

Atrium, Wepf Verlag, Basel, 1985

Architektur im Möbel/
Furniture as Architecture,
Waser Verlag, Zürich, 1985

Mies van der Rohe – less is more,
Waser Verlag, Zürich, 1986

Fantasie in Holz/Fantasy in Wood,
Birkhäuser Verlag, Basel, 1987

Myron Goldsmith – Bauten und
Konzepte/Buildings and Concepts,
Birkhäuser Verlag, Basel, 1987
Rizzoli Publ., New York, 1987

China – Tao in der Architektur/
China – Tao in Architecture,
mit C.K. Chang,
Birkhäuser Verlag, Basel, 1987

Architecture de Chine,
avec C.K. Chang,
Edition Andr, Delcourt, Lausanne, 1988

Tempel und Teehaus in Japan/
Temple and Tea-House in Japan,
neue Auflage/new edition,
Birkhäuser Verlag, Basel, 1988

Santiago Calatrava, Ingenieur-Architektur/
Santiago Calatrava, Engineering Architecture,
Birkhäuser Verlag, Basel, 1988
2. erweiterte Auflage, 1990
span.-engl. Lizenzausgabe,
Editorial Gustavo Gili, Spanien, 1989

Richard Meier,
Building for Art/
Bauen für die Kunst,
Birkhäuser Verlag, Basel, 1990

Tadao Ando, Sketches/Zeichnungen,
Birkhäuser Verlag, Basel, 1990

Ernst Koller 1900–1990,
Kontraste eines Konstrukteurs,
Krebs-Verlag Basel, 1990

Norman Foster, Sketches,
Birkhäuser Verlag, Basel, 1991

Helmut Jahn, Airports,
Birkhäuser Verlag, Basel, 1991

Bauen vor der Stadt/Suburban Buildings,
mit Dieter Wronsky,
Birkhäuser Verlag, Basel, 1991

Orient/Occident,
Beton Verlag, Düsseldorf, 1991

Fügen + Verbinden/Joint and Connection
Birkhäuser Verlag, Basel, 1992

Chicago Architecture –
Holabird & Root 1880–1992,
Birkhäuser Verlag, Basel, 1992

Weishaupt Forum – Richard Meier,
Birkhäuser Verlag, Basel, 1993

Norman Foster, Sketch Book,
Birkhäuser Verlag, Basel 1993

Mies van der Rohe – Die Kunst der Struktur
Mies van der Rohe – The Art of Structure,
Neuauflage
Birkhäuser Verlag, Basel 1993
The Whitney Library of Design,
New York, 1993

Tomsk, Texture in Wood/
Texture en Bois/Textur in Holz,
Birkhäuser Verlag, Basel, 1993

Transformation – Livio Vacchini,
Birkhäuser Verlag, Basel, 1994

Restaurants Paris Belle Epoche
Waser Verlag, Zürich, 1995

Richard Horden – Light tech
Birkhäuser Verlag, Basel, 1995

Holz Pionier Architektur
Wood Pioneer Architecture
Waser Verlag, Zürich, 1995

Helmut Jahn
Transparency/Transparenz
Birkhäuser Verlag, Basel, 1996

Stein Pionier Architektur
Stone Pioneer Architecture
Waser Verlag, Zürich, 1996

Metall Pionier Architektur
Metal Pioneer Architecture
Waser Verlag, Zürich, 1996

West Meets East – Mies van der Rohe
Birkhäuser Verlag, Basel, 1996

Richard Meier, Details
Birkhäuser Verlag, Basel, 1996

Mies van der Rohe, Studiopaperback
Birkhäuser Verlag, Basel, 1996

Renzo Piano, Museum Beyeler
Benteli Verlag, Bern, 1998

Werner Sobek
Ingenieur-Kunst/Art of Engineering
Birkhäuser Verlag, Basel, 1999

Mies van der Rohe, Farnsworth House
Birkhäuser Verlag, Basel, 1999

Mies van der Rohe,
Lake Shore Drive Appartments
Birkhäuser Verlag, Basel, 1999

Tadao Ando
Museum der Weltkulturen im Rhein
Vice Versa Verlag, Berlin, 1999

West is East is West, Mies van der Rohe
Vice Versa Verlag, Berlin, 2000

Ernst Koller – Erfinder und Konstrukteur
Investor and Designer
Wepf Verlag, Basel, 2000

Begegnungen
An Architect meets Architects
Birkhäuser Verlag, Basel, 2000